EMPLOYEE COMMUNICATION
THE STRATEGIC APPROACH

A practical manual including real life documentation
from some of the UK's most successful organisations

LIZ COCHRANE

THE INDUSTRIAL SOCIETY

First published 1997 by
The Industrial Society
48 Bryanston Square
London W1H 2EA
Tel. 020 7479 2000

Typeset by: GCS
Printed by: Formara Limited
Cover Design: Form Graphic Design

The Industrial Society is a Registered Charity No. 290003

ref. 1517TW2.2001/1

contents

preface

This manual was conceived at an Employee Communications Association advisory group meeting in Spring 1996. The Association aims to share best practice and to advance core skills in internal communication management, so advancing the professionalism of the discipline. As the positive impact of employee communication on business effectiveness is better understood, interest has grown in how employee communication practitioners can add value by operating at a strategic level. The Association receives more and more enquiries about how organisations identify communication needs; how they develop strategies and plans, and how they measure success.

This manual is one of the ways that the Association is responding to that thirst for information. The content addresses the way that employee communication managers are acting as internal consultants in a thoroughly practical, down to earth way, rooted in the experience of over twenty organisations.

We were fortunate to have Liz Cochrane as "midwife" for the manual. Liz is a member of the advisory group for the Association and has extensive experience as an employee communication manager, including eight years within Glaxo. She has spoken on various aspects of internal communication and has also written on the subject. Her personal knowledge of developing communication strategies and plans against a background of continuous change both informed the research she undertook with communication managers, and added value to the final product.

Communication is the lifeblood of any organisation. Having the opportunity to facilitate improved communication up, down and across a company, helping to underpin change and achieve business objectives, can be challenging, exhilarating—and sometimes frustrating! The more we pool our experiences and share our learning, the better we will be able to serve our companies and the poeple in them—so ultimately contributing to the health of the economy and to society overall.

Jenny Davenport
Product Development Manager
The Industrial Society

foreword and acknowledgements

This book has been written as a result of the help of a large number of communication practitioners who were kind enough to spare me their time in the Spring and Summer of 1996. I had embarked on a project to gather examples of "live" documentation used by practitioners who are acting as internal consultants to their organisations. It soon became apparent that the real value of this exercise was not simply the documents, but the advice, hints and tips which formed the stories behind the pieces of paper.

The book is a collation of advice, mini case studies of strategies that had been employed prior to my research, and documents. In some cases the comments made are clearly attributed to one individual. But as many of the themes that developed were reiterated by a number of the professionals I spoke to, I have amalgamated the majority of comments for ease of reading. However, all that follows is thanks to the generosity of the people I interviewed in sharing their experiences learning.

Thanks are also due to the following, for providing me with contact names and with ideas for the bibliography: Eileen Scholes of the ITEM Group plc; Andraea Dawson-Shepherd of Hedron Consulting Ltd; Andrew Lambert of People in Business; Colette Dorward of Smythe Dorward Lambert; Jenny Davenport and Paul Davis of The Industrial Society and Richard Varey of the BNFL Corporate Communications Unit at Salford University. From these individuals I gathered more leads than I could possibly follow through in the time available — testimony to the quality of work currently underway in the world of internal communication.

May I also thank my colleagues on the advisory group of the Employee Communications Association for their help and support, with a special reference to Dominic Walters of Austin Knight for penning the chapter on "Getting the most from external consultants". Finally, thanks to the management of Glaxo Wellcome Operations for their help and support while I was researching the book.

list of contributing organisations

Automobile Association — *Phillipa Stokes*
Andersen Consulting — *Craig Smith*
BT — *Teresa Ford*
Bass Taverns — *Anna Foster*
BBC — *Alaric Mostyn*
BNFL Fuel Division — *Peter Osborne*
The Boots Company — *Nicholas Wright*
The Body Shop — *James Harkness*
Cable and Wireless Business Networks — *Jane Mullins*
Cellnet — *Jennifer Johnson*
Digital Equipment — *Susan Robbie*
Glaxo Wellcome Operations — *Liz Cochrane*
ICL — *Laura Ferguson*
Inland Revenue — *Nicola Walters*
Lloyds Bank — *Paul Rudd*
Lombard Personal Finance — *Sarah Fasey*
London Borough of Redbridge — *Paul Williams*
The Tetley Group — *Debbie Standish*
National Grid — *Trevor Seeley*
National and Provincial Building Society — *Paul Chapman*
Nynex — *Adrian Seward*
PACE Ltd — *Roy Johnson*
Parcelforce — *John Payne*
Post Office Counters — *Harry James*
Royal Mail (Anglia) — *John Newson and team*
The Royal Bank of Scotland — *Peter Casebow*
Unipart — *Frank Nigriello*

introduction

- This book has been compiled following a series of interviews with managers across a wide range of organisations who are responsible for internal communication. It aims to provide practical examples of the approach they have taken to being effective internal consultants and moving internal communication forward in their companies.

- The book contains a combination of documents developed by and used in organisations, together with hints, tips and examples of how the documentation has been produced.

- Internal communication is a relatively new discipline. In 1995, Clutterbuck Associates & Business Intelligence Ltd studied the current state of play in the way internal communication is supporting organisational change. The "Is anyone listening?" survey was carried out across major UK organisations. Of 248 responses by self identified internal communication practitioners, only 22% said that their function had existed for more than five years.

- A survey of employee communication by the Industrial Society in 1994 as part of the Managing Best Practice series identified that 55% of the 915 organisations who responded employed someone with specific responsibility for employee communication. Of these, just under two thirds worked within personnel with 15% reporting direct to the chief executive. 14% were part of corporate communications or PR. At that time, only 29% of respondents had written communication policies, and just one in three linked employee communication to the company's strategic plan.

- However, as the importance of effective internal communication to support change and the achievement of business goals grows, so the role of the internal communication practitioner is changing. Rather than simply writing the internal staff newspaper, or managing the mechanics of the team briefing process, the internal communication person is increasingly being called on to be an internal consultant, providing advice and guidance to the organisation and a strategic approach to communication that directly supports business objectives. This book looks at four key areas which are vital for success in this internal consultancy role:
  — developing relationships with customers
  — identifying customer needs

— developing communication strategies and plans
— evaluating effectiveness

Suggestions are also made on the effective use of external consultants.

- As the nature of the job market changes, so people are becoming personally responsible for their development and their careers. We no longer rely on the organisation we are employed by to take career decisions on our behalf. Research by Andrew Lambert of People in Business indicated that a significant proportion of internal communication practitioners see the job as a temporary staging post in their careers. This means it is increasingly important for the internal communication person to manage their role in a way which develops robust communication in their company, while also increasing their personal experience and developing general managerial skills which will be useful in their future career. These skills could include strategy development; project managing a plan from conception to implementation; and monitoring and evaluating success.

- IMPORTANT HEALTH WARNING. Every organisation is unique. A strategy, plan — or even an approach — which has worked in one company at a particular time cannot simply be reproduced in another in order to achieve the same results. Every solution must be tailored to the needs and culture of the specific organisation. However, when approaching a new task it is valuable to gain an insight into what different organisations have done — and more fundamentally, how they did it.

1 developing customer relationships

The internal communication professional can only have a positive impact in their organisation by working through others. Success depends on:
— *taking time to understand the demands facing the organisation and individual managers, then demonstrating how you can help achieve business objectives*
— *adding value at both a tactical and a strategic level*
— *learning to challenge effectively*
— *having clear definitions for the role of the internal communication practitioner and line managers, and ensuring that appropriate processes are in place to support managers as the key communicators in a business.*

Qualities of the internal communication practitioner

- Frank Nigriello, Group Communications Director of Unipart describes the role of the internal communication practitioner as both an advisor and implementer.
  — Advisor: because the internal communicator should **challenge** accepted wisdom, and ensure that situations are seen from different perspectives, and in the widest possible **context**.
  — Implementor: because the communicator's professional skills should provide a workable **solution** to the most intractable communications problem.

- So what kind of qualities does the internal communication consultant need in order to add value to their organisation? Contributors to the book thought the following important:
  — personal integrity
  — networking and developing strong relationships
  — challenging effectively
  — tenacity
  — assertiveness
  — hunger for information: internal and external
  — assimilation, interpretation and analysis of information

— seeing the wider picture — so that messages can be put in context
— presenting a range of viewpoints
— presenting cases coherently to senior management
— professionalism and expertise
— not being a glory seeker: ensuring that others "own" the ideas.

Developing credibility

- The internal communicator needs a high level of credibility to be able to challenge, and to have advice and suggestions accepted. How can this be achieved?

- Some organisations select their internal communication champion by identifying a line manager who is already highly credible having delivered results in another part of the organisation. The manager of the "Understanding Process" in the National and Provincial Building Society (now merged with Abbey National) was recruited this way because her key task was to challenge the "Direction Team" whenever she thought that they were acting in conflict with what the company was trying to achieve.

- Get the support of the Chief Executive Officer or equivalent. Spend time exploring how your skills can help him/her achieve business objectives. Some practitioners develop a personal communication plan with him/her, ensuring that the plan is linked to the organisation's business objectives and that the messages to the various audiences inside and outside the organisation are clear and aligned. Once you have the commitment and backing of the CEO, you can begin to work with other managers.

- If you are not immersed in up-to-date business knowledge of your organisation, take time out to understand the demands facing your managers and people and the objectives they must meet. Go on the road with sales reps: spend time on the production line; join your purchasing people in meetings with suppliers. Do it on a regular basis. Become a generalist in your approach to business, rather than a specialist. This ensures you understand the needs and the constraints of your customers so you can add value to the business by challenging in an appropriate way and giving advice that will help your customers achieve their objectives.

- Find time to meet with key people in the business. Listen to them. Understand their needs, and the needs they perceive the organisation to have. Make sure that you understand:
  — their role
  — where they fit in the organisation
  — what they are contributing to the business
  — what they see as their communication needs/ how you can support them.

- Avoid esoteric, theoretical discussions with customers. Use the opportunity of solving practical problems both to build your credibility and to increase people's understanding of effective communication. Make sure that you are available to customers when they need your help.

- Develop a relationship with customers that extends beyond work issues. Take time to ask them about their home life. One communication manager keeps an aide memoire in the shape of an organisational chart on which she notes key details about customers, their children's names, where they are going on holiday, etc. Another makes a policy of seeing people outside work time — discussing issues over dinner in a less formal environment.

- Don't spend your time exclusively with managers. If you are genuinely going to represent a range of perspectives, you need to understand what those perspectives are. Rather than relying exclusively on the results of surveys and other measurement tools to base your understanding of what is important to the people throughout your organisation, find opportunities to talk with them. Build in their needs and perspectives to the communication strategy.

- If you aim to be perceived as an advisor rather than a doer — find an area where you can offer immediate advice to a key customer to demonstrate your judgement — but don't offer to implement the solution on their behalf. Pass the responsibility for making it happen back to the appropriate line manager.

- Demonstrate by the questions you ask and comments you make that you are focused exclusively on your customer and their needs. Understand their perspective. Work through their problem with them. Help them identify how they can solve it.

- Avoid taking the credit for an effective solution. Ensure others "own" ideas and projects. Remember — you are the kingmaker not the king!

- Find opportunities for "quick wins" to build credibility and to demonstrate the contribution you can make to the business. Identify an immediate need that will help your customer achieve their objectives — then provide the solution. This could be as simple as planning and implementing a series of CEO letters for an organisation that lacks any communication on business direction from the top. The important factor is that the solution provides tangible, measurable, business improvements.

- Having won credibility through delivering results — or preferably in tandem with doing so — work on the long term strategy for communication. But avoid focusing exclusively on the long term without delivering immediate results. Most organisations aren't that patient. They want to see an immediate return on their investment in you!

Within six weeks of joining the organisation, Craig Smith, head of internal communication for Andersen Consulting, a worldwide firm of management consultants, converted the in-house journal from print to an electronic version run on Lotus Notes. Advantages included:

— the ability to "customise" the newsletter — targeting relevant information at specific audiences

— the opportunity for readers to call up additional background information and access business data relating to the story on their screens

— substantial cost savings

— the ability to monitor the profile of readership of articles by grade, country and organisational group.

- Don't bite off more than you can chew. Be clear on who your key customers are. Focus on providing them with an excellent service. Make sure you can stay close to them and understand their business needs. Several companies reported that they have recently restructured to have a small communication unit at the centre, plus people with a responsibility for communication in each operating division. This allows the local people to be close to their customers and understand their needs.

- Business crisis is often the time when communication comes into the sharpest focus. A number of communication practitioners commented that their profile had increased significantly during a time when the business faced its most significant risks. Using your specialist knowledge to recommend how best to communicate raises your profile and credibility. Two companies interviewed commented that following such circumstances, the role of communication has been enhanced and is now seen as an integral part of the company's management process. Members of the communication team now regularly attend and play a full role in meetings of the company's "top team" and are part of key project teams.

- Make sure you pay sufficient attention to the deliverables and to getting the simple things right. You may be a brilliant strategist, but if a name is spelt wrong in a newsletter, or a helpline number is not answered, your credibility will suffer.

- Building relationships is a bit like painting the Forth Bridge — a never ending task. If a key customer leaves and is replaced — you need to do it all over again.

Challenging effectively/avoiding conflict

- A key role for the communication practitioner is to challenge the thinking of others — often at senior levels in the organisation. Other potentially daunting tasks include coaxing an intransigent manager about the value of communicating, or persuading an overly enthusiastic customer that the video he/she has set his/her heart on may not be the best solution to his/her communication needs. So how can you tackle these situations while maintaining strong relationships?

- Rule number one: use the business knowledge you have gained from spending time with your customers. If you link a challenge to a business objective — for your customer or the broader business — you are much more likely to succeed. By being a generalist rather than a specialist, you will be better able to identify with your customers, identify potential issues, and position your point of view from the perspective that it is the best way of achieving a business objective. Being seen as a help rather than a hindrance goes a long way in winning people over!

- Remember — one of the most important parts of your role is to see a situation from a range of perspectives. This is where you can really add value to customers, who may well be focusing on the project they have to deliver without linking it to other things that are happening in the business. Help them to think through the implications of yesterday's announcement of record profits by your plc on the communication they must make on capping overtime payments. Encourage them to get into the mindset of the people they will be communicating with. What factors will influence how people receive the communication? This is challenging your customers' thinking — in order to achieve the best outcome for them and for the business.

- Use challenge to protect the credibility of your customers. One communication manager interviewed recalled a major change planned for her organisation. She wrote a series of questions — covering all issues staff were likely to be concerned about. She passed these to the project team to answer. Where she perceived that the responses provided were inadequate she challenged the team on whether they were taking the right course of action using the principle that if you can't explain it, you shouldn't be doing it.

- Before challenging on any issue, do your homework. Analyse relevant data. Internal sources might include survey material or results from focus groups. External information could include press cuttings, information from trade associations or other relevant bodies on factors which could influence the issues under debate. If you don't have any facts to back up your point of view — go out and find some. Talk to other people and get their perspective. Arguments which are well thought through and based on facts rather than feelings are more likely to win the day — particularly in organisations with a strong data rational approach.

- Keep it simple. Choose key facts that support your argument and focus on those. You are more likely to gain understanding and commitment to your viewpoint.

- Always prepare in advance for meetings with customers — particularly where you are aiming to influence them. Make sure you can understand their perspective. What is important to them? What are their priorities? Their values?

Doing this will go a long way to avoiding potential conflict. Some communication practitioners use a simple checklist, such as:
— what do I want to achieve from this meeting?
— what is the benefit to the customer?
— why might they be resistant?
— what other priorities might they have?
— will they trust me? (if no: what can I do to build their trust)

- Help people to come to their own conclusions about the most effective approach to a communication challenge by structuring their thinking for them. "Customer (originator) research framework for developing a communication programme", a document developed by Parcelforce and included in the identifying needs section, is an example of how structured questions can be used to guide a customer's thinking.

- Ensure that you have strong backers in the organisation. Win their support by initially focusing on supporting them and solving their communication needs, as described above.

- Identify role models and use them effectively. Find opportunities for your communication stars to influence their peer group — and to explain how their approach to communication is helping them achieve their objectives. One organisation organised regular "communicator lunches" for line managers from different business areas following a communication training programme rolled out across the company. These both helped resolve a lateral communication issue identified by course participants, and provided a forum for sharing communication problems and learning from each other.

Responsibilities of the communication consultant vs. line manager

- Clarity of responsibility between the internal communication consultant and line manager is key both to ensuring the effectiveness of communication in the business and the sanity of the communication practitioner. It is neither practical nor appropriate for one person or unit to shoulder responsibility for the effectiveness of communication across a company. Responsibility for good communication lies with every manager in the organisation. He or she is critical to delivering messages, interpreting so they are relevant locally; listening and responding to queries and concerns, and generating local involvement and decision making. The communication practitioner is a facilitator, ensuring that processes, competencies and other communication tools are in place, monitoring their effectiveness against agreed standards and helping managers to be as effective as possible through advice, coaching, support and challenge.

The importance of the role of the line manager should never be underestimated. The Body Shop has a range of excellent — and innovative — communication media including print and video. It also has feedback mechanisms that go direct to the top of the organisation such as the Red Letter scheme — where a member of staff can write a suggestion or comment, send it to a director and be assured of a response within forty-eight hours. A voluntary communication network stretches across all departments and shops. The volunteers are provided with core information at a monthly meeting, and are responsible for ensuring that local areas hold regular communications meetings.

However, its first staff survey, held in 1995, showed that there was a need to increase the responsibility of line managers in order for communication to be seen to be more effective by staff. A programme to provide training, include communication in management competencies and increase the ownership of communication by managers has now been started and is already bearing fruit.

- Ensure that the expectations of line managers — and the expectations they have of you — are clearly defined so that there is no ambiguity. Some communication departments draw up customer services charters, specifying the service they provide and the standards they are committed to achieving, and are measured against these. The charter used by ICL is included in the documentation section.

- Where an organisation is large enough to have a central communication unit plus satellite teams, it may be helpful to draw up a service level agreement to ensure clarity on each other's roles. BT — whose agreement is in the documentation — reported that the process used to define the agreement was particularly useful. The different teams came together and worked through what needed to be included and why.

- Different organisations are at different stages in ensuring that managers have full responsibility for communication. Some communication practitioners prepare communication plans in conjunction with their customers. Others provide customers with planning tools and train them in their use. The aim should be to encourage managers to see communication as a fundamental part of their ongoing decision making and planning process.

Paul Chapman, Director, Organisation Design and Development for National and Provincial Building Society, stresses that the role of the communication manager should be to ensure understanding of what the organisation is aiming to achieve and how, rather than to convert people. The task of gaining commitment rests with line managers. Attempts by a communication practitioner to win people over rather than presenting objective facts can result in loss of credibility (the Pravda syndrome). This makes the individual less effective in the organisation.

National and Provincial went through a radical change programme, re-engineering all its processes and rethinking roles and relationships across the company. The size of the communication team was reduced because the change was about releasing the potential of everyone in the organisation and giving them the skills and space to do things for themselves. The role of the communication team was initially to act as mentors, transferring their skills to others. Later, they focused on the logistics of the company's "Understanding Process" (see Chapter Three for details) and provided analysis of the wealth of feedback coming up through the organisation.

- The communication practitioner has a particular role with the senior management team in an organisation — drawing issues to their attention; and effectively holding up a mirror to show the team how they are perceived by others. To do this effectively, the communication person is described by the communication manager for Cellnet as "one enormous ear" — winning the trust of people across the company, and having highly developed listening skills.

Competent communicators

- To be effective communicators, line managers need strong communication skills, and to see communication as an integral part of their role rather than as an add-on. If your organisation uses management competencies, work with your HR department to ensure that communication is a fundamental part of the competency set used for selection and to identify future development needs. Increasingly, companies are measuring managers' ability against the desired competencies through 360 degree appraisal. This means asking an individual's manager, colleagues, internal customers and members of the individual's team to assess the person's ability to use a range of essential skills — and how often the skill is used in practice. Performance against the competencies is sometimes a major factor in agreeing the individual's annual pay increase. Examples of managerial competencies are included in the documentation section.

- Make sure that effective development programmes are in place so that where specific skill gaps are identified, they can be filled. Have a range of delivery methods in place to meet different learning styles. Work with your training and development department to ensure that the solutions developed really meet the needs and that they fit the culture of your organisation. Some companies going through a major culture change programme introduce blanket communication training to ensure a consistency of understanding of what is expected and why, and to start to equip people with the necessary tools. Others use a more targeted approach, identifying the specific skill gaps of individuals and providing solutions.

- Use employee surveys to monitor the effectiveness of the competency development programme. Publicise the progress that is being made and the help that is available.

Real life often means that line managers can be asked to discuss difficult or complex issues with their team before they have had the necessary communication skills training. The key to success here is to provide practical help first, and follow up with the long term development programme once the crisis has passed. With the issue still fresh in the organisation's mind, there will never be a better time to persuade your top team that investing in communication skills is worthwhile!

Parcelforce is a company that operates in a heavily unionised — and fiercely competitive — environment. It faced a potential crisis when changes in working practices to meet customer needs were rejected by union members in a ballot. Having made some changes to the original proposal, the company embarked on a major communication exercise. This placed a heavy emphasis on listening to people's individual concerns.

Every manager held local briefings, using communication material prepared by the centre. But they needed to be able to handle the specific issues raised by their teams and to prevent the briefings from getting bogged down by debate on the detail.

A series of national and regional help desks were established, staffed by HR and supported by the communication team — who designed the process. On receipt of a phone call from a manager, the help desks promised to provide an answer in general terms within 24 hours. The manager would then discuss the specific circumstances with their team. This increased the confidence of managers holding the briefings, while demonstrating that a listening approach was being taken.

Following a second ballot staff accepted the changes to working practices.

Communication skills are now part of an overall set of managerial competencies recently developed. Parcelforce's approach is to provide each manager with a structured document to use to identify his/her development needs. This is personal to him/her. It is shared only with a "mentor" (not part of their management line) with whom he/she will agree a personal development plan.

- To be effective communicators, managers need to understand the broader context in which they are operating — both externally and internally. Without this understanding, it is difficult for a manager to be able to put messages in their fullest context. It is important, for example, to have the necessary knowledge to be able to relate a change the team is facing to external pressures in the marketplace. Designing forums where groups of managers discuss issues on a regular basis with the senior management team is one way of broadening management thinking. Providing a press clippings service, inviting appropriate external speakers, or identifying opportunities for people to spend time with customers can also be valuable — particularly for operations which are not customer facing.

Making sure that managers have the necessary skills to communicate effectively is important but it is not enough on its own. Managers must also see the value of communicating so that they are motivated to make it part of their management style. When The Tetley Group introduced team meetings as one element of a communication strategy, time was spent with every function to understand their business issues and identify how the team meeting process could help them meet their objectives. This was time consuming — it took six months to complete the project in an organisation employing 2,000 people at that time. However, it was a worthwhile investment, building a foundation of real understanding by line managers of what communication could do for them, and ensuring that the team meeting process could be fine tuned to best meet business needs.

- It's not just line managers that have responsibilities. Some companies are now defining the responsibilities that each member of staff has. The Body Shop Bill of Rights and Responsibilities spells out what all staff can expect from the company — and what the company expects in return. Communication is a strong underlying theme.

Documents in this section

DOCUMENT No: 1.1
Organisation   ICL

Document Description: Customer Services Charter
Defines levels of service that internal customers can expect from the Group communication team

Customer Services Charter

Group communications is available to assist all ICL businesses, cross functional heads and internal communications departments, in all matters relating to employee communications. Assistance is available in the following areas; communication plans, communication behaviours, communication competencies for managers, communication policies and strategies, event driven communication such as business changes directly affecting the employee, employee communication campaigns on specific subjects, internal communication audits and measurement systems and communication mechanisms including planning and execution where required of publications, videos, audio tapes, team briefing systems, face-to-face communications and any other required media.

As an internal supplier of such services Group Communications commits to the following:

- All telephone calls will be returned within 24 hours by a member of the Communications team.

- All electronic mail will be responded to within 24 hours.

- All customer requirements for communication services will be responded to by a written brief to be signed off by the customer before work is undertaken.

- All communication project work will have a budget and project end date to be agreed by the customer.

- All customer requirements which need to be outsourced will be tendered to a minimum of two agencies to ensure cost competitiveness, creative input and customer satisfaction.

- All customer inputs and changes will be recorded before being actioned. Where possible, customers should request these changes in writing.

- Prior notification of a minimum of two days will be given to the customer before sign off of the final work.

- All customers will be required to complete a short questionnaire on Group Communications upon completion of a project to assess the success of the department in meeting the above customer commitment.

LC/jw/10002/021096

DOCUMENT No: 1.2

		Description	Agreement between Corporate Relations Department and divisional communication unit (p1)
Organisation	BT		
Document	Service level agreement		

SERVICE LEVEL AGREEMENT

1. AGREEMENT BETWEEN: Corporate Relations Department and BT Divisions/Group HQ units/other major business units.

2. SLA OWNERS: Head of Employee Communications Divisional ECM (or equivalent)

3. DESCRIPTION OF SERVICES: Employee communications

4. REVIEW SLA: At least annually on 1st January; interim reviews as agreed between SLA owners

5. SERVICES TO BE PROVIDED BY CRD:

    To produce a company-wide Employee Communications plan and guidance for the production of Divisional (or equivalent) and local EC plans.

    To provide a programme of company-wide events and messages for inclusion in Divisional and local EC plans; to update the programme regularly.

    To produce and deliver company-wide EC programmes directly to targeted audiences on behalf of ECQC members.

    To provide integrated, company-wide communications briefings which specify the objectives of the briefing, the target audiences, recommended channels to be used and the timing of release for Divisional/local delivery; advance notice to be given and any pre-release validation to be provided.

    To provide Divisional and local ECMs with copies of all press cuttings and news releases.

    To measure the effectiveness of company-wide communications and channels used, to improve the quality of future communications and to share best practice; to provide guidance on measuring the effectiveness of divisional and local communications.

6. TO BE PROVIDED BY DIVISIONS AND EQUIVALENTS:

    To produce Divisional and local EC plans, based on CRD EC plan and guidance.

    To provide information on Divisional events and messages which may develop into company-wide or public communications.

    To deliver company-wide messages in line with CRD recommendations and to advise CRD of cases where this is not appropriate.

    To measure the effectiveness of communications and channels and to provide timely feedback to CRD to enable continuous improvement.

    To establish SLAs as appropriate with local ECMs and with Corporate Relations Managers (CRMs).

DOCUMENT No: 1.2
Organisation BT
Description Service level agreement (p2)

7. **KEY OBJECTIVES:**

To communicate with our people in a planned and consistent manner.

To produce information which is relevant, comprehensible and timely.

To keep our people fully informed on company-wide and public issues.

To improve communications by monitoring effectiveness and by identifying and sharing best practice.

8. **MEASURES OF PERFORMANCE:**

CARE: company-wide employee communications targets.

Cost reduction targets for publications portfolio.

SLA review.

9. **ESCALATION:**

Day to day issues will normally be resolved between the appropriate CRD EC Account Manager and Divisional ECM (or equivalent).

General issues of concern will be raised at monthly CRD and Divisional ECM meetings.

Intractable problems to be resolved between CRD/CCEC and Divisional ECM or between DCR and Divisional Personnel Director (or equivalent) as appropriate.

DOCUMENT No: 1.3

Organisation Parcelforce
Document Customer (originator) research framework

Description A checklist used by communication practitioners with internal customers when developing a communication programme (p1)

CUSTOMER (ORIGINATOR) RESEARCH FRAMEWORK FOR DEVELOPING A COMMUNICATION PROGRAMME

A. WHAT?

1. What is the budget for the programme?

2. What do you feel you need to say?

3. What is the perception of others? Who have you spoken with?

4. How do these perceptions match?

5. What are the objectives of the programme (what are we trying to achieve)?

6. What is the nature of the message?

Long	Political
Short	Behavioural/attitudinal
Simple	Managerial
Complex	Financial
Sensitive in any way	Legal

7. What is its priority rating?

Crucial	Useful
Important	"Nice to do"

PS0212.DOC

DOCUMENT No: 1.3	Organisation Document	Parcelforce Customer (originator) research framework (p2)

8. What is its purpose?

To persuade	To reassure
To motivate	To promote (a scheme)
To instruct	To team build
To raise awareness	To seek information
To inform	To seek participation
To develop	

B. WHO?

9. Who is the customer (target population) for the message?

   - primary customer/s:

   - secondary customer/s:

10. What do they know already?

    - primary customer/s:

    - secondary customer/s:

11. What are their feelings about/perceptions of the subject now?

12. Do other PO businesses need to know? If so, how much/what?

13. Who will deliver the message?

PS0212.DOC

DOCUMENT No: 1.3

Organisation Parcelforce

Document Customer (originator) research framework (p3)

C. WHEN?

14. When is the best time for the message to be conveyed? (eg. is the climate conducive to its appropriate impact?)

15. What else is planned that might detract from/conflict with/support/build on/etc. the message?

16. When might the message be conveyed to the customer (target population)?

17. How can we ensure an optimum time?

18. What time of the day/week/month/year?

D. WHERE?

19. Where will be message be conveyed?

Admin accommodation
Rest Room
Conference/Meeting room, etc.

E. HOW?

20. How should the message be conveyed (ie. what media are most appropriate)?

21. How much time is available for delivery of the message (eg. do we need more than one session)?

22. How recently was proposed media last used? Is this a problem?

PS0212.DOC

DOCUMENT No: 1.3	Organisation Document	Parcelforce Customer (originator) research framework (p4)

23. Is it planned to use them again in the near future? Is this a problem?

24. What are the other influences over this message?

   The grapevine
   Unions
   Attitude/situation of line manager(s)
   Effects of corridor meetings
   Effects of change

25. What control do you have over these influences? Remember:

   ⊃ The more reliable and timely the information, the weaker the grapevine

   ⊃ The greater the perception of honesty/openness/reliability of the message, the greater the chance of success

   ⊃ Generally, messages should aim to be realistically optimistic

   ⊃ The effects of change have a predictable sequence. This is often characterised by seven phases:

     - immobilisation (being overwhelmed)
     - minimisation (trivialising or denying the change)
     - depression (when the realities are faced)
     - accepting reality (beginning to let go of the past)
     - testing (how I will behave/cope in the new situation)
     - seeking meanings (about how things are different and why)
     - internalising (these meanings and incorporating them in my behaviour)

F. FINALLY

26. Think again: what are the objectives of the exercise?

PS0212.DOC

DOCUMENT No: 1.4

Organisation Inland Revenue
Document Communication Competencies

Description Part of a competency framework containing eight core competences and one specialist one (p1)

MANAGING PEOPLE

We understand what is expected of us and work together productively, in a manner consistent with IR Values, towards achieving our objectives

	STANDARD 1	STANDARD 2	STANDARD 3	STANDARD 4
Outcome:	People manage themselves and their work in the most productive way	People are managed and motivated towards achieving individual, team and the Revenue's objectives	People in the office understand their own and the Revenue's objectives and take responsibility for achieving them	People contribute to achieving the Revenue's objectives across the Executive Office/Division/Revenue as a whole
What the job needs:	1. recommends and agrees personal objectives with own manager	1. defines and communicates parameters and frameworks for individuals and the team	1. discusses and agrees business direction in line with overall Revenue objectives and communicates it to all	1. provides the strategic direction for the Executive Office/Division/Revenue in line with Revenue objectives and ensures it is understood by all
	2. plans, prioritises and organises own work and time to deliver agreed individual and team objectives	2. plans and manages the work of the team ensuring that standards are maintained	2. discusses and agrees work/quality standards ensuring that people understand and maintain them	2. monitors work across the Executive Office/Division/Revenue as a whole through managers to ensure that standards are maintained
	3. works with the team agreeing responsibilities and making best use of skills and experience	3. agrees individual/team targets and shares accountability for achieving them	3. monitors the work of teams to ensure that targets are achieved	3. agrees and monitors targets and is accountable for results across the Executive Office/Division/Revenue as a whole
	4. identifies own development needs and takes positive steps to meet them	4. develops individual/team competence and encourages people from diverse backgrounds to develop their full potential	4. discusses, advises on and arranges appropriate training and development for individuals and teams	4. encourages managers in the Executive Office/Division/Revenue as a whole to develop skills and potential fairly and consistently

DOCUMENT No: 1.4

Organisation Document — **Inland Revenue** Communication Competencies (p2)

MANAGING PEOPLE

Outcome: We understand what is expected of us and work productively together in a manner consistent with IR Values, towards achieving our objectives

	STANDARD 1	STANDARD 2	STANDARD 3	STANDARD 4
	People manage themselves and their work in the most productive way	People are managed and motivated towards achieving individual, team and the Revenue's objectives	People in the office understand their own and the Revenue's objectives and take responsibility for achieving them	People contribute to achieving the Revenue's objectives across the Executive Office/Division/Revenue as a whole
What the Job needs:	5. helps people with problems that they raise and shares the benefit of own experience	5. gives advice and guidance appropriate to individual/team needs	5. takes final decision where necessary on problems raised	
	6. contributes to team decisions and takes positive action to support them	6. leads team meetings and encourages full participation in team discussions and ownership of team decisions	6. chairs formal meetings ensuring agendas are adhered to and appropriate decisions taken	6. chairs meetings/committees which impact across the Executive Office/Division/Revenue as a whole, ensuring agenda· are adhered to and appropriate decisions taken

DOCUMENT No: 1.4
Organisation   Inland Revenue

Document   Communication Competencies (p3)

ORAL COMMUNICATION

Outcome:	We obtain and present information clearly, using knowledge and experience to support our views			
	STANDARD 1	**STANDARD 2**	**STANDARD 3**	**STANDARD 4**
	Factual information is obtained and clearly communicated, according to well defined guidelines	Information is obtained and presented in a manner which is clearly understandable	Complex issues are clearly defined and explained concisely and logically	Issues with wide ranging implications are communicated in a way which is most likely to gain acceptance
What the Job needs:	1. identifies what customers/ colleagues want by questioning and listening to obtain factual information	1. determines the needs of customers and colleagues through careful questioning, listening and analysing of responses	1. establishes customers/ colleagues needs through detailed discussions of complex issues	
	2. gives accurate, relevant and up-to-date factual information to colleagues/customers, clearly and concisely	2. communicates specialist information in a way which can be easily understood by customers/colleagues	2. communicates the interpretation of diverse and complex information logically and clearly	
	3. asks colleagues/manager relevant questions to obtain guidance when in doubt	3. discusses own recommendations for proposed course of action on non-routine issues	3. informs colleagues of proposed course of action on complex specialist/ operational/policy issues	3. seeks and co-ordinates views from authoritative sources within and outside the Revenue and presents findings and conclusions clearly and concisely
		4. conducts meetings in a professional and courteous manner	4. represents own part of the Revenue in a professional and convincing manner in discussions with external bodies and representative groups	4. represents the Revenue as a whole in a professional and convincing manner in discussions with external bodies and representative groups

DOCUMENT No: 1.4

Organisation Document   Inland Revenue Communication Competencies (p4)

WRITTEN COMMUNICATION

Outcome: We produce well written documents that record information and set out recommendations/decisions clearly

	STANDARD 1	STANDARD 2	STANDARD 3	STANDARD 4
Outcome:	Factual information is clearly recorded and communicated, according to well defined rules and procedures	Information is recorded accurately and presented clearly	Complex specialist/operational/policy issues are clearly explained	Complex issues which impact across the Revenue are clearly explained
What the job needs:	1. keeps records up to date, paying particular attention to detail 2. ensures that written information is carefully and systematically filed and can be easily retrieved 3. keeps accurate notes of important conversations and discussions so that a record of relevant information can be clearly understood by colleagues 4. prepares standard forms/letters and communicates routine information neatly and accurately	3. writes clear and concise notes of meetings/interviews, recording accurately what took place 4. drafts non standard letters and memos so that information is conveyed clearly to customers and colleagues	3. writes clear notes of meetings/interviews using own discretion to summarise what took place and the options, recommendations and decisions discussed 4. drafts non standard letters and memos presenting complex specialist/operational/policy matters logically and accurately to customers and colleagues	4. drafts non standard letters and memos presenting complex legal, financial and political information logically, concisely and persuasively to customers/colleagues

DOCUMENTS

DOCUMENT No: 1.4

Organisation Inland Revenue

Description Communication Competencies (p5)

WRITTEN COMMUNICATION

Outcome: We produce well written documents that record events and set out recommendations/decisions clearly

	STANDARD 1	STANDARD 2	STANDARD 3	STANDARD 4
	Factual information is clearly recorded and communicated, according to well defined rules and procedures	Information is recorded accurately and presented clearly	Complex specialist/operational/policy issues are clearly explained	Complex issues which impact across the Revenue are clearly explained
What the Job needs:	5. writes clear and complete reports/submissions/briefings setting out all relevant information correctly and presenting own recommendations	5. writes clear and complete reports/submissions/briefings interpreting and presenting specialist information correctly and explaining range of options and own recommendations	5. writes clear and well ordered reports/submissions/briefings interpreting and presenting complex specialist/operational /policy matters and the range of options/recommendations/ decisions with authority and persuasion	5. drafts politically sensitive reports/documents to senior officials/ministers on complex issues which have implications across the Revenue 6. communicates policy decisions on complex issues which impact across the Revenue in a manner which is clearly understandable

DOCUMENT No: 1.4

Organisation Document: Inland Revenue Communication Competencies (p6)

INTERPERSONAL SKILLS

Outcome: We deal with each other and external customers in a business like, helpful and persuasive manner, that is consistent with IR Values

	STANDARD 1	STANDARD 2	STANDARD 3	STANDARD 4
	People support one another and are courteous to customers	Customers and colleagues are dealt with in a professional manner	Complex issues are discussed and resolved in accordance with the Revenue's views	Issues which have a major impact on the Revenue are resolved
What the Job needs:	1. works as part of a team/teams, being helpful and supportive towards colleagues			
	2. respects the contribution, skills and opinions of colleagues and considers them positively	2. encourages commitment to the objectives of the Revenue by frank and open communication and by encouraging and recognising achievement		
	3. shares ideas and information openly with colleagues and gives them honest feedback	3. discusses difficult/sensitive issues with colleagues and ensures the needs of all parties are considered		
	4. remains courteous and helpful, but firm when under pressure	4. displays tact, diplomacy and firmness when dealing with demanding customers/advisors/colleagues		
	5. uses discretion in determining how to gain the best information from customers/colleagues	5. interviews/negotiates with customers/advisors/colleagues on specialist matters	5. leads difficult, complex negotiations which require the interpretation/enforcement of policy/legislation/regulations	5. leads major negotiations, within and outside the Revenue, ensuring that views and interests are clearly understood and taken into account

DOCUMENT No: 1.4

Organisation   Inland Revenue

Document   Communication Competencies (p7)

INTERPERSONAL SKILLS			
Outcome:	We deal with each other and external customers in a business like, helpful and persuasive manner, that is consistent with IR Values		
	STANDARD 1	**STANDARD 2**	**STANDARD 3**	**STANDARD 4**
	People support one another and are courteous to customers	Customers and colleagues are dealt with in a professional manner	Complex issues are discussed and resolved in accordance with the Revenue's views	Issues which have a major impact on the Revenue are resolved
What the Job needs:	6. establishes and maintains a range of useful contacts within the Revenue/outside bodies to obtain or give factual information	6. develops constructive working relationships with colleagues in other parts of the Revenue/ outside bodies, to collect or explain information		6. consults with other parts of the Revenue/outside bodies to gain support for proposed course of action on complex specialist/operational/policy matters
		7. formally presents information in a well ordered and persuasive manner	7. formally presents complex information in a well ordered and persuasive manner	7. advises and influences senior officials/ministers and gains their confidence and professional respect

DOCUMENT No: 1.5 Organisation PACE Ltd	Document Description	Self Assessment Questionnaire Questionnaire developed for internal consultants in a major building society by PACE Ltd

PART 1   SELF-ASSESSMENT QUESTIONNAIRE

Please study the following scenarios and assess each according to its relevance to your current job and your current level of ability in this skill area.

	RELEVANCE TO JOB					ABILITY				
	Lo			Hi		Lo			Hi	

Helping a client to understand the process and component skills of effective interpersonal communication.	5	4	3	2	1	5	4	3	2	1
Achieving a win-win result in any business discussion that involves persuading or negotiating with other people who have different views and objectives.	5	4	3	2	1	5	4	3	2	1
Establishing a real sense of comfort and rapport in discussion with anyone else, known or otherwise, senior or otherwise, that you need for a business purpose.	5	4	3	2	1	5	4	3	2	1
Ensuring you are in the frame of mind to perform successfully in any important business event.	5	4	3	2	1	5	4	3	2	1
Coaching a client into a new style of thinking about a topic of which you know absolutely nothing.	5	4	3	2	1	5	4	3	2	1
Judging accurately what someone else's point of view is on any topic without their spoken comment.	5	4	3	2	1	5	4	3	2	1
Conducting a consulting interview with a senior manager to persuade her or him of your objective yet unwelcome recommendations.	5	4	3	2	1	5	4	3	2	1

DOCUMENTS

DOCUMENT No: 1.6
Organisation PACE Ltd
Document 360 degree feedback questionnaire

Description Questionnaire developed for senior managers and directors in the property development arm of a blue chip company (p1)

Manager: _____
Giver of feedback: _____
Date form issued: _____ Date form to returned: _____

This form, the inside of which is to be completed, is confidential and will only be seen by you, and the consultancy responsible for the development of this process.

USER NOTES

What is it for?

360° Feedback will enable me to get direct feedback from people I work with - my manager, peers and subordinates. The feedback focuses on communication, the subject of a course that I will attend. Feedback I, and others attending the course, receive before and after the course will be a measure of its effectiveness. The content of the course will be based on a consolidation of the feedback received before the course by all those managers involved.

How do you use it?

There are three stages to 360° Feedback:

First, agree to give feedback. Second, complete the form. Finally, return the form by _____

Who else is involved?

Apart from those giving feedback, will discuss consolidated feedback with me and PACE, the training consultancy, will do the consolidation and design and run the Communication Skills course based upon the consolidated feedback. Only you, and the consultancy will see the form that you complete. I will see only consolidated feedback.

Helpful hints

Giving feedback is challenging. Be frank and fair in your rating and stick to specific examples to back up your rating.

COMPLETION INSTRUCTIONS

Please give a **rating** for me against each of the communication skills dimensions on the following pages.
- The rating runs from 4 at the high end to 1 at the low end. The extremes of the scales are defined.

For each dimension, please also give a specific **example** to support your rating.
- Focus on what you have seen or heard - behaviours. Feedback of this sort is easier to act on and easier to accept because it is non-judgmental.

It is important that you focus on strengths as well as areas for improvement. It is a mistake to focus exclusively on a person's weaknesses. A **balanced** impression of behaviour is needed.

Please ensure that all sections on this form have been completed, in particular the sections at the top of this page.

When completed please return the form to:-

Roy Johnson
PACE
2 White Mark Farm
Hill Road
Watlington
Oxon
OX9 5AF

DOCUMENT No: 1.6   Organisation Document   PACE Ltd   360° feedback questionnaire (p2)

Positive Indicator   **Negative Indicator**

Develops rapport quickly and with a wide variety of people. Listens to others and shows understanding for what they are saying. Is quick to notice, and explore when appropriate, underlying feelings that may be unexpressed. Incorporates and reconciles conflicting views. Appreciates people for their expertise.

Responds in a manner that retains empathy and rapport and, when it is necessary, delivers bad or unwelcome news in a way that maintains people's self respect.

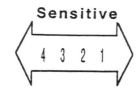

Rarely develops rapport. Often does not listen or show understanding. Is slow to notice, and explore when appropriate, underlying feelings. Does not easily incorporate and reconcile conflicting views. Does not show appreciation for those with technical ability.

Delivers bad or unwelcome news in a way that is unlikely to maintain people's self respect.

Specific example to support your rating_____

_____

_____

Expresses goals and ideas in a way that is easy to understand and digest. Does not confuse with a mixed message. (Readily distinguishes between when she/he is clear and when she/he is unclear.) Asks questions that get to the heart of the matter and expose the available information and flaws. Knows when to stop talking so that the message can be assimilated.

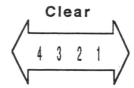

Goals and ideas often expressed in a way that is difficult to understand and digest. Confuses with a mixed message. Questions tend to be superficial. Talks when it would be more useful to be quiet.

Specific example to support your rating_____

_____

_____

Marshals ideas into a convincing and cogent case and delivers this case in a manner that is persuasive and attractive to listen to. Structures concepts logically, visually and verbally. Expresses vision in a compelling manner, unclouded by rhetoric. Engages the commitment and enthusiasm of others. Engages and influences people's values.

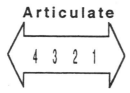

Often does not make a convincing and cogent case. Delivery may be dull and unconvincing. Concepts are sometimes not structured logically, visually and verbally. Vision is either unclear or clouded by rhetoric. Unable to engage the commitment and enthusiasm of others. Does not engage and influence people's values.

Specific example to support your rating_____

_____

_____

DOCUMENT No: 1.6

Document 360° feedback questionnaire (p3)

Organisation PACE Ltd

Adapts to fulfil the role necessary to enable a board or team to work well. Tailors the message to suit different people's competence, confidence and aspirations, and the way in which they think. Helps others to see negative events and opinions in a more positive light to facilitate the way forward to a constructive solution. Adapts quickly to setbacks and misunderstandings to re-think and restate position. Prepared to change position based on feedback and new ideas, which she/he actively seeks.

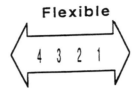

Flexible

Tends to stick rigidly to one style; not adapting to fulfil the role necessary to enable a board or team to work well, or tailoring the message to suit different people. Often colludes with people's negative opinions. Knocked off balance by setbacks and misunderstandings. Sticks to position regardless of feedback, which is rarely sought.

Specific example to support your rating_____

_____

Takes responsibility for the outcome of communication. Focuses on the resolution of problems in a manner that takes into account the overall best interests of all appropriate parties, rather than finding scapegoats. Communicates personal values and those of the company consistently and, when appropriate, own underlying feelings in a way that is believable.

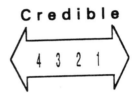

Credible

Focuses on only a limited range of interests when resolving problems. Tends to blame others for problems. Does not communicate personal values and those of the company consistently. May not communicate underlying feelings even when appropriate.

Specific example to support your rating_____

_____

Communicates the wider business context for actions and decisions. Has the ability to stand back, taking and communicating a dispassionate view when others are reacting too hastily to pressure. Focuses on the merits of a case after careful analysis rather than short term subjective feelings.

Strategic

Limits communication of the business context for actions and decisions to own interest area. Tends to be too involved to see the wood for the trees and reacts emotionally when a dispassionate view is needed. Focuses on short term subjective feelings rather than the merits of a case.

Specific example to support your rating_____

_____

Builds a network of partners and alliances inside and outside the company. These alliances may be formal or informal. Creates trust, confidence and a co-operative frame of reference. Is accessible to people and interested in what they have to say.

Affiliative

Does not have a wide network of partners and alliances inside and outside the company. Tends to distrust others and create conflict. Not accessible to people and not interested in what they have to say.

Specific example to support your rating_____

_____

DOCUMENT No: 1.7

Organisation The Body Shop

Document Bill of Rights
Description Bill of Rights and Responsibilities

The Body Shop Human Resources Mission Statement

The Human Resources mission of The Body Shop to its employees is:

To create and sustain a successful community of individuals actively committed to meeting each other's needs.

By this statement we recognise:

• that by **successful** we will achieve our business goals, in terms of both profit and values

• that a **community** has a common purpose in which there is a sense of belonging and security

• that **individuals** are not only accepted but also encouraged to contribute their own unique qualities and aspirations

• that by **meeting each other's needs** we ultimately achieve all of our objectives, we create an environment where there is mutual trust and respect, and we will sustain the successful community

We recognise that there are **rights** and **responsibilities** of both individuals and the community, and these are framed into a "Bill of Rights and Responsibilities"

The Body Shop Bill of Rights and Responsibilities

The Rights of the Company

To make the final decision.
To recruit the best people for the job.
To dismiss people when justified.
To expect a high level of contribution, performance and commitment.
To expect respect for its values.

The Responsibilities of the Company

To do its best to provide a secure environment for its employees.
To look for new ways of doing things.
To educate employees about the Company's culture and values.
To educate employees about the Company's business.
To provide adequate induction and training.
To consider existing employees first when looking at new opportunities.
To meet all relevant employment legislation.
To be honest to employees about what we are offering.
To listen, care and support.
To be fair.
To walk the talk.
To say thank you.

The Rights of the Individual

To have a voice, to challenge.
To have equality of opportunity.
To be trained to do your job.
To be developed as an individual.
To be rewarded fairly for the work you do; to understand how your pay is determined.
To know how the business is doing.
To be told the truth about things that will affect you.
To have a piece of the action.
To have the opportunity to do your best.

The Responsibilities of the Individual

To think.
To learn.
To be honest.
To try your hardest, to do your best.
To treat others with trust and respect.
To take responsibility for your own actions.
To acknowledge the efforts of others.
To obey the rules.
To stand against injustice.

This Mission Statement and Bill of Rights and Responsibilities is the driving force for everything we do, and is the yardstick against which the Human Resources function, and the Company Culture function, and indeed The Body Shop as a whole, can be measured in its dealing with its people.

It covers all aspects of the Human Resources function from Training and Development to Pay and Remuneration, from Recruitment to Pensions, from Induction to Appraisals, from Equal Opportunities to Administration systems.

It recognises and publishes the special nature of The Body Shop's relationship with its employees, in which they are not just resources for the Company, but are people whose own needs and aspirations are recognised and taken seriously.

At its heart is the phrase "meeting each other's needs" which in four words incorporates virtually the whole of our behaviour and actions whilst working at The Body Shop.

14

2 identifying customer needs

A range of tools can be used to identify the needs of specific customers and of the organisation. A vital element for success is to think through the implications and likely resource requirements of actioning the results before beginning the process, and ensuring the commitment for action is there. Raising expectations by involving a customer (whether a senior manager or the whole organisation) in identifying their needs, then failing to deliver for whatever reason, will lead to disillusionment.

Having initially identified needs, involve as many people as possible in the action planning process. This will both ensure ownership through the organisation, and the best results.

One-to-ones

- Rule number one: You need a deep understanding of the organisation, the environment in which it is operating, and the aims to which it aspires, before you can successfully identify needs. Chapter one gives tips from communication practitioners on how to increase general business understanding.

- If you are new to a business, start by visiting and talking with key customers. Use the time to understand their role; where they fit in the organisation and the contribution they are making. Prompt them to talk about their perception of key issues facing the business — and their area. Begin to identify what their communication needs might be.

- Some communication practitioners develop structured question lists to use as prompts for these discussions. Others prefer to let the discussion develop naturally. The choice comes down to personality and the culture of the organisation in which you are working. Examples of question lists are included in the documentation section.

- If you discover discrepancies between members of an organisation's top team about the company's purpose — don't be tempted to use communication to paper over the cracks so that others in the company don't see them. Where fundamental differences occur, it is essential that the team resolve them. Ideally, if they have the necessary skills, the team should go through the process of clarifying their direction themselves — to have total ownership of the outcome. Alternatively, use a facilitator (internal or external) who can design an appropriate process.

- Analyse what your customers say. They may find it hard to articulate what they want to achieve through communication and so tend to focus on immediate needs, such as processes to let people know what is happening across the organisation as a whole. Identify the most appropriate ways of meeting those needs and deliver them — but continue to monitor and focus on the deeper, cultural and behavioural issues which will form the bedrock of your communication strategy.

- Don't take statements about a desire to move to a more empowering or innovative management style at face value. Check out what is being put in place in other parts of the system to make them become a reality. For example, what changes are being made to the way managers manage and appraise their people? Is there a genuine desire to change behaviour at the top of the organisation? If "empowerment" is simply an empty badge or slogan, putting communication processes in place to support it will be counterproductive for the company — and frustrating for you.

> One communication manager reported that she quickly identified some immediate needs within weeks of joining her new company, and put a series of CEO letters and a newsletter in place. Within three months, through listening to people, she could see there was a conflict between the messages and the current behaviours displayed. She used this discrepancy as an opportunity to persuade the organisation of the value of a company audit.

Needs identification tools

- A number of tools exist to gather information and identify needs from the organisation as a whole. These include quantitative processes, typically the employee survey, which provide statistical data, helpful in identifying the extent of an issue. Qualitative processes are used to explore issues in more depth, understanding the reasons behind them. Many organisations use focus groups in this way. The most important thing for the communication practitioner is to have a range of adaptable tools in his/her toolkit — and not to be inflexible in their use. One person interviewed for the book reported that the process of gathering information in a previous organisation had been delayed for months — because of a disagreement in the team about whether qualitative, or quantitative, processes should be used first!

- Be pragmatic in your choice of tool for identifying needs. If you simply want pointers for the way forward, you can use a qualitative tool such as focus groups. You should find that clear themes begin to develop within running just a few groups.

- When structuring any questionnaire, ensure that the questions you ask are directly relevant to your organisation (or the project) and its needs. Any audit should be directly linked to the company's strategic direction. Identify the behaviours and attitudes that are essential for success. Define key subject areas for the survey. Each of these should be areas where you have identified you want to take action to improve or which you know are issues for staff. Make sure the issues are both measurable and actionable. Don't overload the survey. Pick three or four key areas where you know the company will have the commitment and the resources to take action afterwards.

- Be sure that you have buy-in to the objectives of the survey before you start — from the top team, and other managers. Position the survey as something that will help them in achieving overall business objectives — an aid, not a threat. Ownership of the survey process by managers means that action is much more likely to follow the survey results.

- Take care to avoid too many people being involved in the design of the detail of a survey. It is important to get agreement to the objectives of the survey and the main areas to be covered. Other people getting involved in the precise wording of questions may prove to be less than helpful if internal politics start to get in the way of clarity.

- Once the draft survey is complete, imagine the answers. Will it tell you all you need to know ? Redraft as necessary.

- Following up a quantitative survey with focus groups can be a good way of overcoming the problem of people focusing on figures and statistics, rather than on real issues. Involve managers in focus groups — or in team discussions to get under the skin of the findings. Make sure that they have the necessary listening and facilitation skills first.

Focus groups can meet more than one objective. One communication manager described how she ran a series of focus groups to dig under the surface of issues identified through a quantitative survey. Each group was made up of a diagonal slice of the organisation — from different areas and levels. The groups were facilitated by directors. The structure of the groups helped overcome two phenomena identified in the survey. Directors were perceived as being distant. The company was also affected by the 'unknown plonker syndrome' — people from one area did not know the contributions that other areas were making, and therefore did not value them. Providing the opportunity to listen to one another began the process of breaking down barriers. The output of the groups was used to help build the communication strategy, meaning that people felt involved in the process.

Thinking through the process

- Whether embarking on a quantitative or qualitative survey, take time at the start to plan every part of the process. As a minimum you will need to:
  — identify the objectives of the survey
  — formulate the questions
  — pilot the questions, to make sure that people understand them
  — rewrite the questions (less important for a qualitative survey where the facilitator can check understanding during the session)
  — print the survey (for quantitative questionnaires)
  — publicise the survey: explaining what is happening and why
  — organise the logistics
  — invite people to attend a session or
  — for postal surveys: ensure you have an up-to-date list of staff locations
  — carry out the survey
  — analyse the results
  — publicise the results
  — action the results
  — let people know the action you have taken.

- When inviting people to take part in the survey, ensure they understand why the survey is being carried out, how you will feed the results back to them, and what will happen as a result (i.e. what process will be followed to action the results). Also stress the steps that are being taken to ensure the confidentiality of their response.

- Confidentiality is important if you are to be sure of getting people's genuine views — except in companies with very high levels of openness and trust. Even if you have the skills to design a quantitative survey in-house, it is worth employing an external company to administer the survey and process the results. Publicise this, and stress the measures being taken to ensure individual confidentiality — for example, that the smallest size group whose views will be fed back to the company is ten, assuring annonymity.

- Publish the survey results. If you don't, people will assume that they are worse than they are.

- Regular quantitative questionnaires are a valuable way of monitoring the success of change programmes. Make sure your survey includes a core of "benchmark" questions directly linked to the key things you need to achieve as a business. But take care in using normative data, in other words direct comparisons with what other companies score for the same question. Many external organisations who offer a survey service will provide this data. But unless the other companies have been carefully selected because of the similarity of their purpose, strategies and competitive situation, the fact that they are achieving higher (or lower) scores than you may simply not be relevant.

- Most importantly, make sure that the organisation has thought through in advance what process it will put in place to action the findings — and that the necessary resource will be available. There is nothing more counterproductive than to ask people for their views then seemingly to ignore what they say.

Ensuring action and buy in

- It makes sense to structure surveys so that the results can be broken down and thus produce tailored reports for different areas of the business. This makes the results more meaningful and actionable. Spend time talking through the results from each specific area with the appropriate director or management team — as well as addressing the issues coming from the overall survey with the Board or Executive group.

- A company-wide survey and resultant company wide action plan can seem remote. Involving teams at a local level in action planning will help give the process validity in their eyes, and support one of the key principles of empowerment: that the most effective solutions come from within the organisation.

The BBC went through an intensive process to identify needs when starting on its major change programme in the early 1990s. A change management team was formulated — including senior representatives from internal communications, human resources, management development and the Chief Executive Officer.

The initial task was to hold one-to-ones with Board members, to research their views on the purpose of the organisation, its principal strategies and its brand — the essence, or values of the BBC.

Next, a rigorous survey was carried out, to gather perceptions of every aspect of the organisation. These ranged from the degree of understanding and commitment to company goals, to management behaviour, to the effectiveness of current communication tools. This survey used an organisational model founded on the assumption that employee commitment and motivation produce enhanced performance. The model linked internal and external factors, a particularly important factor for the BBC.

Once the results of the survey had been received and an initial analysis had taken place to identify what the data showed, an intensive involvement programme began. This involved the top 250 managers in the corporation. The way in which this was carried out depended on the degree of interest and enthusiasm of individual managers. Formats ranged from formal presentations from the management group, to structured workshops involving business games and role playing.

Next, every manager was mandated to discuss the results with his or her team. They were provided with a suggested process and timetable, and given the task of identifying:

> — up to six actions in their remit which would help their team achieve its objectives
> — three actions at divisional level
> — and one action at Board level which would help them do their jobs better.
>
> This was followed by a discussion at Board level resulting in a commitment to improve in five areas. Local initiatives were prominently publicised through the internal media — to demonstrate what people were able to achieve.

> The Body Shop carried out their first social audit in 1994/95. This covered 10 key stakeholder groups, including employees. The Ethical Audit department — part of head office staff — developed the methodology and carried out the audit, involving other staff focus groups in identifying the issues to be targeted, and at the piloting stage.
>
> Once the results were independently analysed, the head of each corporate area was responsible for developing their individual ideas on necessary actions. These plans then went to the Management Committee and the Main Board for final sign off. After publication, staff had the opportunity to give feedback on the audit results and give their input for departmental action plans. They could do this either by discussing local implications with others in their own department or, if they chose, by looking at company-wide issues at a series of voluntary discussion groups.
>
> The output of this discussion was fed back to the audit team who will report on progress towards agreed action plans and next step commitments made in the first statement. The continual cycle begins again with a second audit in 1997.

- Establishing a working party is an alternative way of getting wider buy in to the actions following a survey. This group is likely to be cross functional and represent a broad sweep of the organisation. This can be a valuable mechanism, ensuring that a range of perspectives and operational requirements are brought to bear when proposing ways forward. However, it is important that the group is made up of people who are going to be forward looking and focus on solutions, rather than to hold a post mortem on the results.

- When publicising the results of a survey or the action plans that follow, take care that communication is not treated as a stand alone feature. Actions being taken to improve communication should be shown to be integrated with other managerial or business improvements taking place.

- Having identified a potential solution to a particular tactical need, it can be helpful to pilot it. The Inland Revenue identified a number of communication issues from a staff survey and a follow up communication audit, including staff who were flooded with paper, and potential inconsistency of messages. One solution identified was to introduce a single regular management publication, summarising all the main issues which all staff needed to know about. This was then used for the basis of team discussions. The publication was introduced gradually across the Department, so that feedback from staff on its content and style could be incorporated at each stage to demonstrate a listening approach and to make sure the solution met employee needs.

- Having taken action as a result of a survey make sure people know what has been done, and that it was linked to what they said. Without prompting, people may not make the connection. Demonstrating that people's views have been taken on board is a great way of building trust.

The Royal Mail Employee Relations team in East Anglia initiated an internal communication campaign to highlight actions being taken following a national staff survey in Autumn 1995. The campaign, called "Plan It/Do It", aimed to involve teams in the action planning process. All teams had the overall results of the survey communicated to them, together with the results for their area. A series of communications followed, highlighting specific aspects of the survey and making recommendations on how to approach a people satisfaction plan. Teams were encouraged to mark the progress they were making, through display on noticeboards, posters and in team meetings.

Royal Mail carries out surveys every six months. Responses for East Anglia in Spring 1996 improved by approximately one third — with 73% of non-managers and 89% of managers responding — the best response rate in the country.

Documents in this section

DOCUMENT No: 2.1

Organisation	ICL
Document	Question List

Description Developed for use by communication practitioners in structured one-to-ones with senior managers

1)   Who are your target audiences?

2)   What 3 key messages do you want to give those audiences and are the messages different for each target audience identified?

3)   Why do you want to communicate to these audiences?

4)   How regularly do you intend to communicate to them?

5)   Are you looking for understanding/involvement? What do you want them to 'do' differently when you've communicated to them?

6)   How are you going to demonstrate that you mean what you say?

7)   What are you trying to achieve by communicating;
a) In the short term?
b) In the long term?

8)   What are your preferred communication styles and methods?

— informal   — structured   — slides   — face-to-face
— formal   — unstructured   — video   — paper based

9)   How do you think you are perceived by your target audience?

10) What external CEO's/companies do you consider to be role models in communications?

11) What difficulties do you think you are likely to encounter in delivering your communications plan/objectives?

12) What support do you think you will need to deliver your communications objectives/plan?

Cable & Wireless Business Networks
Internal Communications Audit

Discussion Group Topic Guide

(2 hours allowed for group discussions - involving 5 - 8 participants in a group)

Part I

Contracting:

- Explain background/purpose of research
- Clarify objectives of session
- Explain roles/responsibilities of group members
- Set and agree ground rules
- Introductions

Part II

Lead-in questions for other Group companies employee discussion groups:

1. How would you describe your role? (relationship with Business Networks)

2. What information do you need to do your job effectively?

3. How would you like to receive that information?

4a. What are some of the things we do now that you would like to see continued?

4b. ...or could be improved?

Lead-in questions for Business Networks employee discussion groups:

1. If your organisation could be likened, to an animal, what would it be?

2. If a mate asked you in a pub what communication is like at CWBN - how would you describe it?

3. Think about someone in this organisation who you think is a good communicator. What do they do that makes them good?

4. What would we like communication to help us achieve?

5.   Let me take you back to the pub again - and someone asks you what your company is trying to achieve and how is it going about it? What would you answer?

6a.   Describe how a team works together when communication is good.

6b.   Describe it when communication is not so good.

Part III

Close:

- Individuals select top three priorities (using post-it notes)
- Agree Group's top three priorities
- How to be kept informed of progress
- Feedback on the session itself

DOCUMENT No: 2.2	Organisation	Cable and Wireless Business Networks
	Document Description	One to one prompt sheet For interviews with senior managers (p3)

Cable & Wireless Business Networks
Internal Communications Audit

One-to-One Interview Prompt Sheet

- One-to-one interviews to be conducted with senior managers from within Business Networks and from other Group companies, who have close regular liaison with Business Networks.
- Allow 20 minutes minimum for interviews.

1. What do you want communication to help you achieve?

2a. What types of information do you need in your role as a team member?

2b What types of information do you need in your role as team leader?

3. What are the most effective channels by which you and your team could receive that information?

4. If I was to ask one of your team to describe your communication style - what do you think they would say?

5. Which of your communication skills might you like to enhance?

6. What sort of things would you like to hear more about from your employees?

7. How do you find out how well people understand what you communicate?

8a. Can you give some examples of things that have worked particularly well?

8b. Can you give some examples of things that have not worked so well?

9. How should we measure how effective communication is?

10. Are there some things that you would like to be doing now that we [*communications function*] can help you with?

11. Are there some things that you would like to take more responsibility for now?

12. How would you describe the style of communication that best aligns with our mission and values?

DOCUMENT No: 2.2
Organisation Cable and Wireless Business Networks

Document

Appendix to audit report. The
Hedron Communication Hierarchy
is reproduced by kind permission of
Hedron Consulting Ltd. (p1)

Communication - A Common View

In reading the outcome of the communication audit, it is helpful if we can work with a
common view of communication, as communication means many different things to
different people. We have found it useful to use the ©Hedron Communication
Hierarchy, which is a simple model of communication, and one which will enable us to
consider communication in its broader sense.

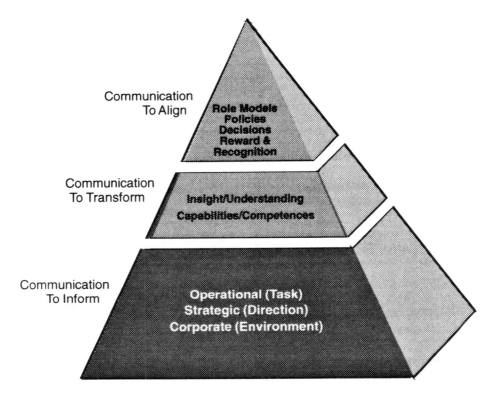

©: Hedron Consulting Limited

Level One - Communication To Inform

The model builds up from a base of what is people's most common view of
communication: information, where most of our conscious communication effort and
budget go. There are three categories:

1.   **Operational** - information which everybody needs day-to-day to get their
jobs done: "what are my objectives?"; "information I need in order that I can make a
decision".

2.   **Strategic** - "strategic" from the individual's perspective. This is information
which is emotive, eg the direction of the business, its values, structure, changes etc.
Information where somebody will be asking "What does this mean for me?", "Do I

DOCUMENT No: 2.2

Organisation Document — Cable and Wireless Business Appendix to audit report (p2)

want to be part of an organisation going in this direction?". Because of this personal dimension, strategic information needs to be discussed to ensure both full understanding and accurate interpretation. It does not lend itself to mass written or broadcast communication channels nor E-mail because most of those techniques do not allow face-to-face discussion.

3.   **Corporate news -** information which breeds a sense of belonging, loyalty, a sense of scale and scope of the organisation and which provides context with the rest of the market, eg that somebody gets a CBE, that we invest in charities, do local community activities, that we are 4th or 5th in the league. This type of information lends itself well to mass communication techniques as there is little discussion required.

Level Two - Communication To Transform

Ultimately, we communicate because we want to influence people's attitudes and behaviours, understand what is going on throughout the organisation, and obtain feedback from those dealing with customers to better inform our strategic decisions. In order to use communication as a means of not just influencing but *affecting* people's behaviour and attitudes, those communicating need to have a personal understanding of how they and their message is perceived. They need the skills to do this: active listening, eliciting ideas and negative comment, handling it and being able to pass it back up the line. It involves being able to manage group dynamics (team discussions) and handle conflict. While these might apply more to managers than staff there is also the insight and understanding of staff to be borne in mind. What is their role in the communication process? Or do they have a responsibility to feed back, ask questions, encourage more dialogue in their team, to source the information they want?

Without this level of the triangle the impact of the efforts in the information level is very limited.

Level Three - Communication To Align

However, as we all know the old adage "Do as I *say*, not as I *do*", is only wishful thinking. This issue leads us to the top part of the triangle.

Those who act as role models in the organisation are key. They are not just those in positions of hierarchy, they are often self-selected peers or respected individuals. People will take their communication from what these people *do*. Cynicism and mistrust creeps in when what they *do* is very **different** from what they *say*. This applies to the wider organisation as well. Executive decisions we make, our policies, our reward and recognition systems speak louder about what is important to the business than any words.

DOCUMENT No: 2.2
Document   Appendix to audit report (p3)
Organisation   Cable and Wireless Business Networks

If these are out of line with the types of information communicated at the bottom of the triangle then all that effort and investment is negated or will possibly have a detrimental effect.

Summary

So communication may cover three areas of activity:
- communication to inform or the exchange of information processes.
- communication to transform - the skills needed to communicate well.
- communication to align - the impact of non-verbal communicators on conscious communication.

In this report we feed back the data against these different levels of communication. Useful information came out across all three levels, which clearly indicate areas where we are already performing well and areas requiring improvements.

14

DOCUMENT No: 2.3 Organisation BT	Document Description	About Focus Groups Extracts from a managers guide to focus group research (p1)

ABOUT FOCUS GROUPS

1   What Is A Focus Group?

A focus group is a method for getting people to think creatively and to openly share opinions about a chosen topic.

It is one of the ways in which managers in BT can understand the opinions of their people and how these should influence strategy, policy and its implementation.

The method involves identifying people who are in some way affected by (or interested in) the subject concerned, and bringing a group of them together in a relaxed environment to discuss some of the issues involved.

2   Research Methods Compared

Compared to other methods of data collection, focus groups are notable for their potential to yield rich, qualitative information that can be presented in a lively way (eg by the use of direct quotes).

On the other hand, they are relatively resource intensive, require sensitive handling for maximum benefit and are unsuited to the collection of large amounts of quantitative data.

Whilst it is impossible to be definitive, the table (on the last page of this section) attempts to summarise the pros and cons of focus groups in comparison with some other research methods.

3   Applications For Focus Groups

Among the many applications for focus groups, they can help to:-
* identify the positive and negative features of situations prior to improvement
* anticipate the thoughts, feelings and actions of BT people when planning new initiatives
* reveal preferences for, or against, alternatives being considered
* test out reactions to new policies and products and services before they are introduced

DOCUMENT No: 2.3

Organisation BT

Document   About Focus Groups (p2)

* identify potential barriers to implementation and look for creative ways to overcome them
* obtain feedback about programmes during roll-out so that subsequent stages can be adjusted
* evaluate activity once completed; learn lessons for future improvement
* improve employee involvement and participation in company decision-making
* identify issues for inclusion in quantitative research (e.g. survey design)
* help to explain the reasons behind quantitative research findings.

Focus group research can play a part at virtually any stage in the introduction of a product or service into BT. In designing the focus group it is important to be clear about the purpose of that particular phase of data collection.

4   Characteristics Of Focus Groups

Focus groups can be characterised by the following attributes:-

Non Directive: There is at least some freedom for the discussion to follow its own direction and generate unexpected, but potentially useful interpretations

Safe Conditions: The success of a focus group depends on creating the kind of environment in which people feel comfortable (physically and emotionally) and are willing to share their views honestly and without fear of retribution

Internal Dynamics: The stimulus for the discussion is generated internally within the group, not just by the questioner; people respond to one another and the method exploits these interactions

Creativity: Were it not for a creative component the focus group might be better described as a "group interview". The method allows for people to develop ideas as they go along, building on the views expressed by others. Participants are encouraged to think laterally and suggest improvements rather than passively accepting the status quo

Depth: Focus groups are intended to delve beneath the surface, to explore people's feelings and to probe their motives, to seek root causes rather than symptoms.

5   Who Should Use Focus Groups?

If you are faced with the need to understand a situation involving people (e g understanding the issues behind your employee attitude survey results), you may find that there are features of the focus group approach which you can use when involving your people in discussion.

If you support line managers in developing the organisation, focus groups can provide a useful way of collecting data on behalf of clients and feeding it back in an absorbing and accessible way.

If you are a professional researcher, focus groups will be an essential part of your armoury of techniques for answering the clients' enquiries, particularly when used as part of a mixed design involving complementary methods.

There is a note of caution however; those of you who regularly use focus groups will be only too aware of the numerous pitfalls and the ease with which the approach can be discredited by thoughtless and unprofessional application.

6   Benefits Of Focus Groups

Although the primary aim of focus group research is to collect data to enhance action planning and bring about change, significant side benefits are often obtained:-

* focus groups are a learning environment that can help people tackle problem solving and can make them aware of people management issues
* focus groups permit people to express their feelings and opinions in depth and at length and this can have a cathartic effect, a feeling of having "got it off my chest"
* bringing people from different work environments together for a common activity helps to reinforce the BT value "we work as one team"
* focus groups are a social activity, allowing people to interact with others and share experiences
* focus groups can help to engender a sense of involvement and participation among those who take part and may be seen by others as a visible demonstration that the company is willing to listen to employee concerns
* those running focus groups have also been known to gain from them in the following ways:
  - social satisfaction from contact with those at the "sharp end"
  - kudos from being regarded as the visiting "expert"
  - enhanced understanding of the issues discussed
  - skills development and job enrichment
  - feelings that they have contributed to a worthwhile activity.

DOCUMENT No: 2.3

Organisation BT

Document   About Focus Groups (p4)

Pros & Cons Of Focus Groups Compared With Other Research Methodologies

focus groups
postal questionnaire
telephone interview (structured)
face to face interviews (semi_____ structured)

	focus groups	postal questionnaire	telephone interview (structured)	face to face interviews (semi structured)
Design expertise required	H	H	H	H
Involvement/exposure for client	M	M	L	M
Time/effort to set up	H	M	H	H
Interviewer/administrator skill	H	M	L	H
Detachment/objectivity of researcher	L	M	H	L
Breadth of issues that can be covered	L	M	H	L
Depth/flexibility of questioning	H	M	L	H
Involvement/interest for participants	H	M	L	H
Learning/development for participants	M	L	L	H
Anonymity for participants	H	H	H	M
Cost/time per participant	H	M	L	M
Ease of analysis and interpretation	M	H	H	L
Meaningful/relevant results	H	M	L	H
Credibility of method with client	M	M	H	M
Generalisability of results	L	M	H	L

Key
H = High   M = Medium   L = Low

DOCUMENT No: 2.4	Document	Communications and relations with managers
Organisation National Grid	Description	Extracts from company-wide employee survey (p1)

Communications and relations with managers

for office use only

12. How far do you agree or disagree with the following statements about how your immediate **supervisor/manager** actually **behaves? If you work for more than one person, please apply this question to the one you consider** the main **person responsible for you and your work.**

He/she:	Strongly agree	Agree	Neither agree nor disagree	Disagree	Strongly disagree	
Listens to my views and problems	1	2	3	4	5	(58)
Acts on my views and problems where appropriate	1	2	3	4	5	(59)
Lets us know how we are doing as a team/working group	1	2	3	4	5	(60)
Consults me before he/she takes a decision affecting me	1	2	3	4	5	(61)
Explains the reasons behind decisions	1	2	3	4	5	(62)
Trusts me to get on with my job	1	2	3	4	5	(63)
Encourages me to make my own decisions	1	2	3	4	5	(64)
Encourages me to put forward ideas and suggestions	1	2	3	4	5	(65)
Regards mistakes as learning opportunites rather than crimes	1	2	3	4	5	(66)
Takes goods decisions	1	2	3	4	5	(67)
Communicates effectively on work issues	1	2	3	4	5	(68)
Regularly lets me know how well I'm doing	1	2	3	4	5	(69)

13. Performance Management is intended to be a joint process between your line manager/supervisor and you. Regular discussion about your work activity and performance progress is an important part of the process.

My manager and I discuss my work activity and performance progress ...?

Never	1	(70)
Sometmes, but not as often as I'd like	2	
Regularly	3	

© The Industrial Society

DOCUMENT No: 2.4	Document	Communications and relations with
Organisation National Grid		managers (p2)

for office
use only

14. Please state which response most closely describes the way in which your performance is measured?

I understand the way in which I am measured, and find
the measures helpful 1 (71)
I understand the way I am measured, but do not find the
measures helpful 2
I know I am measured, but I do not understand how 3
I am not aware that my performance is measured 4

15. How far do you agree or disagree with the following statements about communications between you and managers more senior than your immediate manager/supervisor?

	Strongly agree	Agree	Neither agree nor disagree	Disagree	Strongly disagree	Don't know/not applicable	
I am consulted as much as is practicable about major change in **NGC**	1	2	3	4	5	6	(72)
There are enough opportunities for me to communicate to decision makers how I feel about things that affect me and my work	1	2	3	4	5	6	(73)
People who speak up in **NGC** tend to be labelled as trouble makers	1	2	3	4	5	6	(74)
Managers may listen but they often do nothing about what you say	1	2	3	4	5	6	(75)
Top managers in my **business** are in touch with the views and opinions of staff	1	2	3	4	5	6	(76)
Top managers in **NGC** are in touch with the views and opinions of staff	1	2	3	4	5	6	(77)
Top managers in my **business** are approachable	1	2	3	4	5	6	(78)
Top managers in **NGC** are approachable	1	2	3	4	5	6	(79)
Top managers from my **business** are rarely seen in my unit	1	2	3	4	5	6	(80)
Top managers from **NGC** are rarely seen in my unit	1	2	3	4	5	6	Card 2 (7)

© The Industrial Society

DOCUMENT No: 2.4

Organisation National Grid
Document Action plan in gantt chart
form (p1)

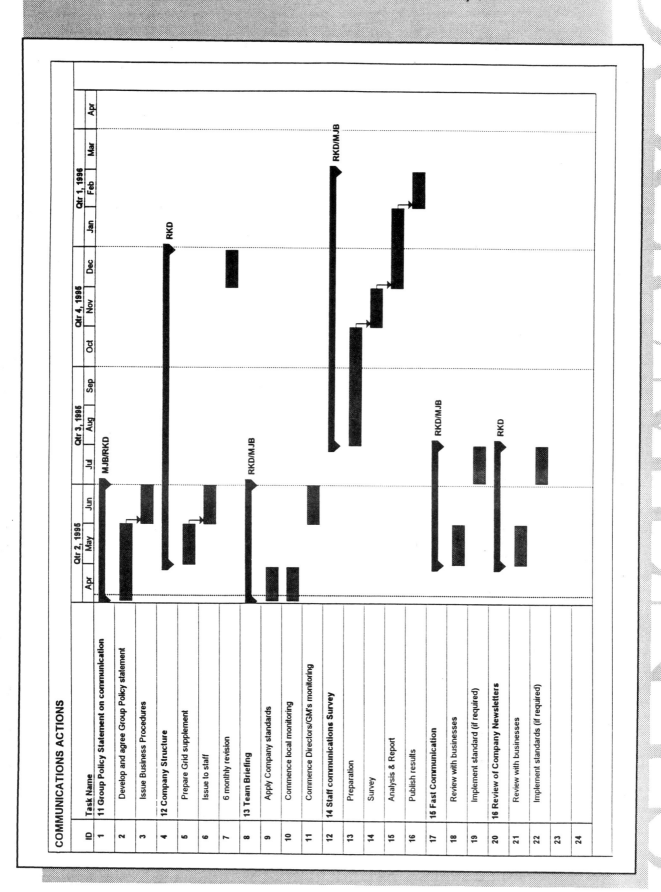

COMMUNICATIONS ACTIONS

ID	Task Name
1	11 Group Policy Statement on communication
2	Develop and agree Group Policy statement
3	Issue Business Procedures
4	12 Company Structure
5	Prepare Grid supplement
6	Issue to staff
7	6 monthly revision
8	13 Team Briefing
9	Apply Company standards
10	Commence local monitoring
11	Commence Directors/GM's monitoring
12	14 Staff communications Survey
13	Preparation
14	Survey
15	Analysis & Report
16	Publish results
17	15 Fast Communication
18	Review with businesses
19	Implement standard (if required)
20	16 Review of Company Newsletters
21	Review with businesses
22	Implement standards (if required)
23	
24	

51

DOCUMENT No: 2.4
Organisation   National Grid

Document   Action plan in gantt chart form (p2)

COMMUNICATIONS ACTIONS

ID	Task Name	Qtr 2, 1995			Qtr 3, 1995			Qtr 4, 1995			Qtr 1, 1996			
		Apr	May	Jun	Jul	Aug	Sep	Oct	Nov	Dec	Jan	Feb	Mar	Apr
25	17 Reform Internal Communication Focus Group						RKD/MJB							
26	Agree terms of reference & members													
27	First meeting of new Group													
28	18 Annual Review Video			RKD										
29	Preparation of script/treatment													
30	Filming													
31	Video sent to staff at home													

DOCUMENT No: 2.4

Organisation Document

National Grid
Action plan in gantt chart form (p3)

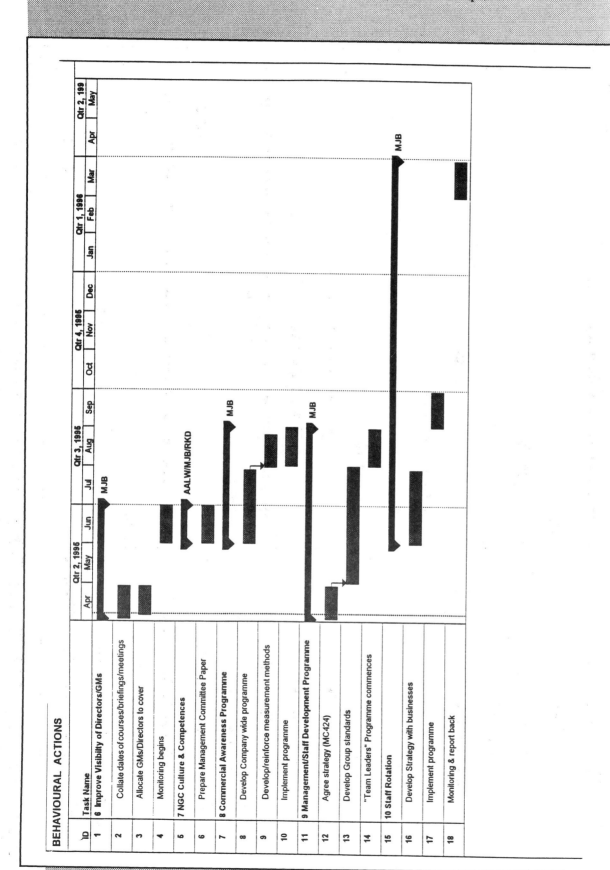

BEHAVIOURAL ACTIONS

ID	Task Name
1	6 Improve Visibility of Directors/GMs
2	Collate dates of courses/briefings/meetings
3	Allocate GMs/Directors to cover
4	Monitoring begins
5	7 NGC Culture & Competences
6	Prepare Management Committee Paper
7	8 Commercial Awareness Programme
8	Develop Company wide programme
9	Develop/reinforce measurement methods
10	Implement programme
11	9 Management/Staff Development Programme
12	Agree strategy (MC424)
13	Develop Group standards
14	"Team Leaders" Programme commences
15	10 Staff Rotation
16	Develop Strategy with businesses
17	Implement programme
18	Monitoring & report back

53

DOCUMENT No: 2.4

Organisation   National Grid

Document   Action plan in gannt chart
form (p4)

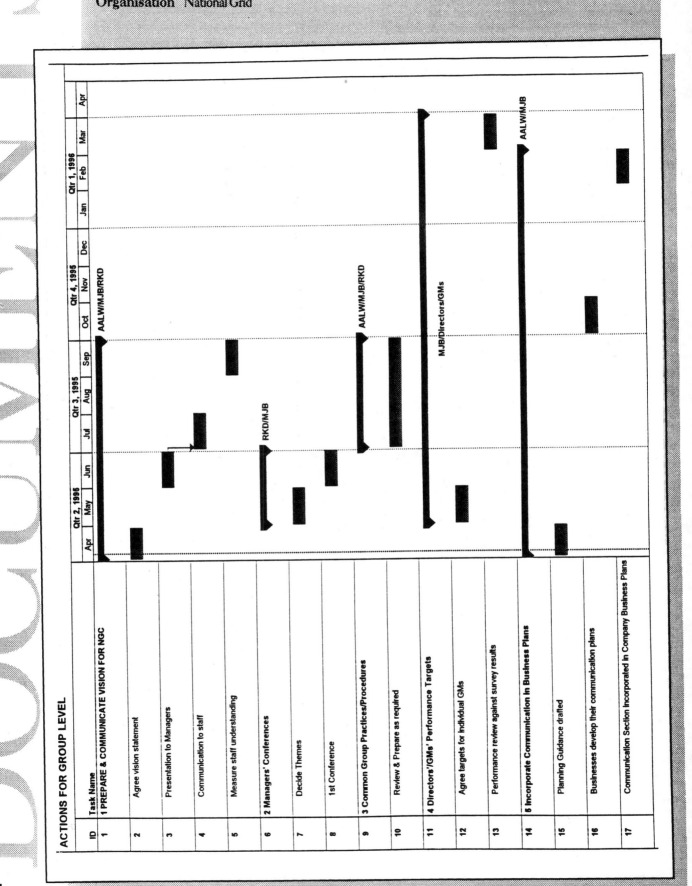

DOCUMENT No: 2.5

Organisation BNFL Fuel Division

Document Description Planning chart
Chart indicating the level of planning required prior to an employee survey

FUEL DIVISION EMPLOYEE SATISFACTION SURVEY - 1995

TIMESCALE	ACTIVITY	ACTION	COMPLETED
6 March	Survey cleared with TU/SS.	A W	
7 March	Survey pilot at FD - 20 employees	PMO to organise RO to conduct	
8 March	Employee numbers by Cost Centre info prepared and sent to RO	PMO	
17 March	Write to Cost Centre managers - details of the survey/organisation/requirements/ return of questionnaire/booking of rooms etc	CAH/PMO	
17 March	Prepare posters/publicity re survey Issue and advertise around site	PMO/Mac	
23-28 March	Surveys delivered to site and issued to Cost Centres. Prepare labels.		
10 April	Surveys returned to RO - Admin post room collection point (by 6 April)	Cost Centre Managers Admin	
28 April	Raw data to DJC for BQA submission	RO	
19 May	Completed. Results due and available.	RO	
29 May	PR Department to consider - issue and format		
	Results issued to Departments/across Site • How? • When? • What? • Who?		

TAB/ADMIN/018-2

DOCUMENT No: 2.5

Organisation Document — **BNFL Fuel Division Survey extract (p1)**

PLEASE READ

Instructions for completing the questionnaire

- *Fill the boxes like this* — *to record your answer. Please use an HB pencil or a black/blue pen. Please do not use red ink.*
- If you make a mistake on an individual question - do not attempt to correct it, draw a line through all the boxes for that question to make your answer void.
- **If a question does not apply to you, please do not answer it - leave it blank.**
- For questions which require an opinion, there is a grid of two to five boxes to show grades of opinion, e.g. from 'Strongly Agree' (box 1) to 'Strongly Disagree' (box 5).
- *Do not* mark your answers like this: ✗ ✓ ⊕ otherwise the computer will not be able to read your answer.

Examples of completed answers

	Strongly Agree	Agree	Neither Agree nor Disagree	Disagree	Strongly Disagree
A01 I am interested in coverage of BNFL in the news media.	=	▬	=	=	=

	Yes	Don't know	No
A09 I understand why BNFL needs to continue to reduce the number of its employees.	▬	=	=

START HERE

PERSONAL DETAILS AND EMPLOYMENT GRADE

All information will be treated in strictest confidence and no individual will be identified by our independent consultants processing the results. Legally, our consultants cannot release information about individuals to BNFL.

Please mark personal details below. These allow us to collect views by grade, gender, age, group etc. Cost Centres are also marked to indicate views by work area. No individual can be identified by any BNFL employee.

Type of Employment

Full Time Days =	Full Time Shifts =	Part Time =	Agency/Contract =

Level of Employment

Apprentice =	Craft =	Non Craft =	Local Support Staff = OL1 (PSR's 1-5, 3-7, 6-10 9-13)
Supervisory Grades = OL2 (PSR's 12-16, 13-17, 14-18, 15-19)	Junior & Middle Management = OL3 (PSR's 18-22, 22-25, 24-28)	Senior Managers = OL4 (PSR's 27-31, 29-33)	Senior Management Group = (SMG and above)

Age

16-25 =	26-35 =	36-50 =	50+ =

Gender

Male =	Female =

Length of Service

Less than 1 year =	over 1-2 years =	over 2-5 years =	Longer than 5 years =

DOCUMENT No: 2.5

Document Survey extract (p2)

Organisation BNFL Fuel Division

Section A You And Communication (questions not applicable leave blank)

Communications - Face-to-Face Meetings

		Very Good	Good	Reasonable	Poor	Very Poor
A01	Overall, I think that communications with employees in our Division are:	☐	☐	☐	☐	☐
A02	Overall, communication between me and my immediate Boss is:	☐	☐	☐	☐	☐

		Yes	Not Sure	No		
A03	I understand where the work of my section fits into the overall business of BNFL.	☐	☐	☐		

		Got Better		Stayed the Same		Got Worse
A04	In the last year, has overall communication for you:	☐		☐		☐

A05 Below are three columns. Column 1 lists various sources of information about BNFL and your Division. We would like you to complete columns 2 and 3.

	Mark ✓ boxes only for the *main* ways in which you think you *currently* get your information	Mark ✓ boxes only for the *main* ways in which you would *prefer* to get your information
The 'grapevine'	☐	☐
Immediate Boss	☐	☐
Internal Memos	☐	☐
Notice board	☐	☐
Trade Union/Staff Unions	☐	☐
BNFL News	☐	☐
Videos	☐	☐
Team Briefing/Monthly Briefing	☐	☐
Site Newsletters	☐	☐
Personal contacts in your own or other departments	☐	☐

		Yes		Not Sure		No
A06	At our monthly briefing we review our section's/team's work performance	☐		☐		☐

		Yes		No		
A07	Does your section/team meet together on a regular basis with your immediate Boss or his/her Boss?	☐		☐		

		Once a Week or More Often	Once a Fortnight	Once a Month	About Once Every Three Months	About Once Every Six Months or Less
A08	If 'Yes' to question A07, how often are these meetings held?	☐	☐	☐	☐	☐

		Always	Most of the Time	Occasionally	Seldom	Never
A09	When questions are asked at these meetings are satisfactory answers given?	☐	☐	☐	☐	☐
A10	Are people's opinions asked for at these meetings?	☐	☐	☐	☐	☐
A11	Do these meetings give you information that helps you do your job better?	☐	☐	☐	☐	☐

3 developing communication strategies and plans

Historically, the internal communication practitioner was a tactician, brought in towards the end of a project to agree how to communicate a business decision. Now the potential of the role has grown enormously, as has the contribution it can make towards the effectiveness of the organisation. This can only happen where communication is a fundamental part of the business planning process, built in from the start, with communication objectives directly linked to business objectives, and where listening is seen as being at least as important as giving information. This requires strategic skills — plus the pragmatism to turn strategy into action.

An integrated, strategic approach

- A company's communication strategy needs to be derived from and intrinsically linked to the overall business goals for the organisation. If there are elements of the communication strategy which do not link in to what the company is aiming to achieve overall, you should question why they are included.

- Communication is one of a company's key tools in moving from where it is now to where it wishes to be in the future. The communication strategy should therefore be directly linked to research findings. Andrew Lambert, managing director of People in Business, comments that very often this is not the case in practice — meaning that the strategy has a lower probability of success.

- A communication strategy will typically include:
  — communication objectives: linked to business goals
  — analysis of research: identifying priority areas for action
  — top level strategies: how improvements will be achieved. These could include:
  — processes for
    - delivering messages
    - feedback

- involvement/empowerment
- lateral communication
— communication competencies: defining behaviours
— communication standards
— key messages or themes
— roles and responsibilities
— measures and measurement processes.

• A range of extracts from communication strategies are included in the documentation section.

• The communication carousel (below) outlines a simplified process linking communication strategies and plans to business need.

COMMUNICATION CAROUSEL

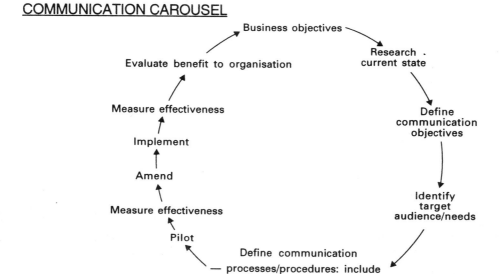

• It is important to get a range of viewpoints when developing a communication strategy. A number of companies set up a steering group to formulate the strategy and subsequently to monitor its implementation to ensure that it continues to meet business needs. In addition to internal communication professionals, these steering groups could typically include:
— representatives from Human Resources and Organisational Development if appropriate
— senior managers with a company-wide perspective: the deputy managing director, company secretary or head of business planning, for example
— the head of public relations (unless the PR and internal communication functions are integrated)
— authoritative and highly respected line managers.

The members of the group need to be committed to the value of communication. Don't include any sceptics at the strategy formulation stage. Though the process could convert them, they will slow the group down and may increase the risk of wrong decisions being taken.

- An increasing number of organisations are integrating communication into every aspect of "the way they do business". The senior member of the communication team is part of meetings of the top team. Typically his or her remit is to represent the perspective of the employee at these meetings, with a brief to challenge other members of the team. He or she will therefore both influence the thinking of the group, ensuring that the implications of decisions taken are thought about at the outset, and will also ensure that decisions on what, how and why to communicate are intrinsic to every stage of the decision making process, and are built into the overall strategy — rather than being hurriedly considered once a final decision has been taken.

- Rather than having a communication strategy, The Body Shop builds communication into each strand of the company's main business strategies. This ensures that communication is an integral part of managing the business.

- Ensuring that members of the communication team join key strategy or project groups is an extension of this integrated approach. Again, this ensures communication considerations can be built in to every stage, while also having the benefit of broadening the business understanding and knowledge of the communication professionals, and giving an opportunity to contribute in other areas. Parcelforce take the opportunity to second junior members of the communication team full-time onto business projects as a development opportunity.

Companies using the European Quality or "Business Excellence" Model have found this has helped to ensure that the importance of communication is recognised — and to position it appropriately as part of the management process. Post Office Counters described how, following adoption of the model, the need for a more integrated approach to communication was recognised, together with a structured, planned approach. Now, local heads of communication sit on each of the regional boards. A communication strategy was defined by the communication team at head office, with input from local communication heads. The strategy has been interpreted into an action plan, held electronically. All communication activity is fed into this, and progress against the plan is monitored on a regular basis.

- One way of making sure that communication becomes built in to "the way we do things around here" is to build it in to every meeting. A number of companies have a standard that every business meeting will include an agenda item to consider what should be communicated (to whom and how) as a result of the meeting.

- Avoid the temptation of acting on preconceived ideas when defining your communication strategy. Always test against the company's needs, and the information that research provides. Nicholas Wright, head of employee communication for Boots, believed that the corporate newspaper was surplus to requirements because of the range of business journals produced by each of the operating divisions and the changing nature of the organisation. However, research demonstrated that staff place high value on belonging to Boots as a parent company — and that the paper provides useful corporate adhesive, complementing the local vehicles. The strategy now adopted by Boots is evolutionary change, reflecting the culture of the organisation.

Using ears and mouths in proportion

- Every communication strategy — and each communication process used in a company — should have a feedback mechanism built in. Listening is probably the most important skill in communicating — and the one that is hardest to get right. Unless formal feedback systems are put in place, the combined knowledge of people in the organisation will be wasted. Real commercial advantage will come from understanding issues and concerns, and liberating ideas across the company, as well as encouraging managers to do the same at local levels. Identifying ways of releasing view and opinions, then harnessing them, is a key role for the internal communication professional.

- Two way communication can take different forms — consulting staff prior to a decision being taken to get their views; listening to their ideas and concerns; involving them in the decision making process. However, even one way communication, where staff are informed of a decision, requires built in listening, to check for understanding and to answer questions.

- Use feedback mechanisms to understand the issues that are of concern to staff then build them into your rolling communication plan. People are unlikely to be prepared to listen to the subjects which the company is concerned about if the organisation is not prepared to reciprocate.

- Listening means you can assess what people heard you say. This may be very different to what you thought you said! We all interpret what we hear in the light of our own experience and expectations. Listening to how people react and respond to a message allows you to reinterpret and clarify as necessary.

- A listening approach doesn't just happen because the right processes are in place. Appropriate behaviours need to be there too. Ensure that company development programmes include listening and facilitation skills and encourage openness. Remember how hard it may be for some managers to listen to and accept challenge and criticism from individuals or in open forums, without reacting negatively or being defensive. Before starting such a programme, coaching to ensure an appropriate style is very important. It may make sense to resource this internally. Alternatively, this may be an area where outside help is useful, particularly when working with a senior management group, who might prefer to practise new behaviours with help and feedback from someone outside the organisation.

- Don't assume that the value of listening will be automatically understood. Do the necessary preparatory work to ensure that managers appreciate the need to take other perspectives on board. One communication manager explained how she took the time to feed back the results of the survey to individual members of the executive team, to ensure that they really understood not only what the results were showing but also that they role modelled the values of listening and facilitation. Then members of the team led mixed focus groups made up of people from across the company, to gain a greater understanding of their perspectives and to get input into how communication could be improved.

- A feedback system needs to include a process for actioning the information that comes back through it. Think this through and put it in place before you ask for feedback. Don't underestimate the amount of time it may take to analyse and action comments.

- Ensuring that action does follow the comments raised is crucial. One of the biggest demotivators is to ask what people think then ignore what they say, or fob them off with bland responses. Encourage managers to put processes in place so that issues are followed through. If no action can be taken, ensure they explain why not — giving the quality of response they would want to receive. The director and general manager for Royal Mail Anglia has regular listening sessions. He incorporates any concerns into his personal development plan.

- Team briefing processes can be adapted to encourage team members to use part of team meetings to identify performance issues — then establish groups to examine problems and come up with recommendations, feeding back progress through the team meeting system.

National and Provincial Building Society (now merged with the Abbey National) went through a radical restructuring in the early 1990s. The result was a business organised along its processes. The company has four processes — Direction; Implementation Management; Implementation, and Understanding. The Understanding Process wraps around the other three, and is designed to ensure understanding of the company's direction and the contribution required from people, and to give everyone an active role in success.

Each member of staff ("team player" in N&P terminology) attends a team event once a fortnight. During this, the team first considers what has gone well or badly and notes any other issues. The focus is on what the team can learn from this. They also consider the aide memoire — a summary of key issues from the direction process — compiled by the top team. The meeting is all about the team taking responsibility for itself and its own success in achieving customer satisfaction. Where issues cannot be resolved by the team, they are referred to a point where action can be taken. Each issue is also noted and sent to a central point: the Opportunities to Improve Team. The responsibilities of this group include logging every issue raised on an "issueometer" and summarising the outputs of every team event into a document which is accessible to all. The issueometer provides an early warning of company-wide issues, allowing speedy action by the direction team (the top team).

Paul Chapman, Director, Organisation Development describes the company's approach to communication: " You have to win hearts and minds, so people understand what and why. Unless there is two way communication, you won't achieve genuine change. Communication is fundamental, to broadening people and to breaking down barriers."

The company developed its radical approach to managing the business by first taking the top team on a five day workshop, where issues were identified; approaches to tackling them agreed, and the next steps for communicating defined. Following this, a cascade of three day workshops covered the whole organisation. Managers' workshops followed a similar format to the Direction team and were hard hitting. Workshops for staff had a softer focus, to ensure staff understood the process, and that the direction team understood the issues staff were facing.

The National and Provincial approach is described in more detail in the documentation section.

- Building discussion groups into the communication matrix can be a useful way of integrating feedback and developing understanding between people in different parts of an organisation. A number of organisations arrange sessions in which people have the opportunity to meet informally with a director or CEO to ask questions and discuss business issues. Added value can be gained where the director uses the opportunity to listen and encourage feedback.

- It can be helpful to provide invitees to discussion groups with a brief in advance. This should state the objectives of the session, and let people know what to expect, and what is expected of them. One communication manager also includes some background facts and figures on the company following feedback that staff would find this useful.

Inside and out - integrating plans

- In addition to deriving directly from a company's business strategy, the internal communication strategy also needs to be closely aligned to — or integrated with — the external communication strategy. It is vital to think of all stakeholder groups when planning a communication. Will the message you plan to give internally send shock waves externally, or vice versa. Many organisations have joint internal/external communication plans, so that the implications of a particular business initiative can be thought through from the perspective of all its audiences. An example of joint internal/external communication planning by Parcelforce is included in the documentation section.

- Timing of major announcements has to be thought through carefully for different stakeholders. Most organisations try to ensure that their staff are the first group to hear important news. This may not be possible for publicly quoted companies where announcements with potential share price implications must be given to the stock exchange first. Here, most try to aim to give the information to staff simultaneously (generally using E-mail or other technological solutions). Explaining to staff as to why some information must be released firstly to the stock exchange is helpful.

Raising the standard high

- Once the communication strategy has been developed, it then needs to be articulated in a meaningful way. A number of companies do this by publishing communication standards. These are typically derived by identifying the gaps between where the company needs to be in its communication approach and style and where it is now, then devising standards which, when achieved will plug those gaps. Performance against the standards is then monitored on an ongoing basis.

Lloyds Bank went through a rigorous process before drawing up its communication standards. This started when grassroots feedback indicated that people were growing increasingly uncomfortable with the change being experienced.

First, the bank initiated research to understand the key issues and their root causes. Focus groups were held to gather people's feelings about the bank, and to identify what they would like to see happen to resolve those issues. Next, a quantitative survey was carried out, to validate the issues and identify how widespread they were.

The results were analysed and presented to the top team, who identified the top issues for attention.

Next, the bank initiated "the debate" in which everyone was invited to participate. Line managers presented the survey results and the priorities for action. They also described the process which would follow. Teams then developed sets of local actions, and made recommendations on what should happen nationally. These were fed to the internal communication team at the centre. They directed issues to different parts of the business for action as appropriate. They also developed the communication strategy — focusing on resolving the remaining issues.

The communication strategy gained the active endorsement of the management team. Next, it had to be communicated — but it was a weighty document. No one would read it all. So the communication team extracted the key areas which could be measured — and drafted the communication standards. But they wanted to make sure that the end result was relevant and accessible.

They initiated a further series of focus groups to test the draft standards and revised them in accordance with comments from staff. This process only finished when the majority view from the groups was that the standards were both understandable (ie not couched in management jargon) and measurable.

Now, progress against the standards is regularly monitored through research. The performance of individual managers against the standards is also assessed on an ongoing basis, and linked to the bank's performance management system.

A copy of the standards is included in the documentation section.

Action planning

- A well thought through communication strategy provides a long term context for communication activities, ensuring that what happens supports the organisation's business objectives and goals. It also provides a framework and structure for activity. But a strategy is no good without action. It is important to have action plans which directly support the communication strategy, ensuring that progress is made and monitored.

- When defining a communication plan, think about different groups, and what needs to be achieved with each one. Awareness and understanding may be sufficient for parts of the organisation with some messages. It may be vital to have the active commitment of other groups. In general, where awareness alone is required, providing the information — and giving opportunities to ask questions and check understanding — will be enough. To gain commitment, a high level of involvement is essential. People buy in to what they feel they own.

- Companies differ in the support given to line managers to develop their own communication plans. Some communication professionals work with line managers and develop plans jointly with them. Others have evolved to the stage where they provide advice and guidance, but the line manager develops his or her own plan. To do this effectively, the manager needs a high level of understanding both of communication and of how to plan.

- BT has a very formalised planning system. Within the company, no business plan submitted for authorisation will be approved — or receive the necessary funding — unless it includes a communication plan.

- There will be times when you need to communicate quickly and there is no time to plan — other than on the back of the nearest envelope. Having clearly defined values, communication standards and key themes are useful here. They provide a useful checklist against which to measure your emergency communication, to ensure the maximum consistency.

- Even when you have time to plan, the chances are that things will change. So, is it useful to plan? Yes — because:

— you can schedule your activities and organise your resources better

— you can liaise with others to agree your expectations of them

— the planning process encourages participants to think through the implications of what will be communicated as far as each stakeholder group is concerned. It therefore flushes out issues at the start

— the plan articulates intentions and gives landmarks and a logical sequence of events. If these are shared, it is easier for the team to adapt and change with circumstances

— developing a twelve to eighteen month integrated message plan, covering all the key messages and actions internally and externally, will flag up any potential clashes — the announcement of a reduction in benefits the week before a customer jamboree, for example. The plan can then be used to raise issues with senior managers, in order to influence and get counter productive decisions or timings changed.

- Rather than including detailed messages in your strategy and plans, agree key themes. At a strategic level, these can prevent you from getting sidetracked by something that seems newsworthy — but doesn't have any strategic importance. At an action planning level, providing managers with key themes plus additional background information will give them a flexible framework to work within for maximum effect. Exceptions to this rule are where absolute consistency is a priority such as in major announcements.

Planning major change

- One of the times when the communication professional is very high profile is when planning for major change. It is important to be an integral part of the process — preferably from the start, so that you can influence people's thinking about how the whole change will be handled. You may be asked to lead a team to plan the communication. If so, construct the team carefully. Make sure you have got a wide range of viewpoints and experience. One communication manager in this position included a change champion and a resistor. She also made sure that a new person, and someone with long service who had "seen it all before", were involved. And she made sure that the team included a woman who had demonstrated a high level of intuitive understanding in the past.

- A key role for the communication person when planning a major change is to challenge. Think of all the questions anyone might ask. Put these to the change team. Get them to answer them. If the answers aren't credible — get them to think through the implications of that. An inability to answer a question could mean that insufficient information is available to take a decision — thus highlighting a key business issue.

Scenario planning is an important part of planning to communicate major change. One communication manager was part of a project team planning the relocation of manufacturing facilities. The announcement was due to be complicated by associated announcements regarding downsizing and capital investment. Final decisions on the shape of all the changes had not been made. The first task of the project team was to map out the communication objectives, messages and implications of each of the options under review. This process helped to flush out issues and so helped the decision making process.

- When communicating major change; make sure that the context is clear — explain why the change needs to happen. Use the time while the change is still being planned to paint a picture of the rationale for staff. This avoids a communication vacuum, and helps to prepare the way for the eventual communication by building understanding.

- It is a legal requirement to consult staff representatives in certain scenarios. For example, where redundancies affecting more than 20 people are contemplated employers are required to consult individuals and employee representatives. Similar legislation requires consultation with employee representatives in takeovers and other transfers of undertakings. Work closely with your HR representatives, who will need to be up-to-date with the legislation, and plan carefully.

- Whenever you communicate change, make sure that feedback channels are in place as early as possible. Understand people's concerns from the outset. That way, you can plan your communication from the perspective of the recipient.

The Royal Bank of Scotland has seen major change in a number of its operations. One particular challenge facing the bank in 1994 was the introduction of a new management structure. This involved every managerial job in the branch network changing. New salary and reward structures were brought in. New competencies were introduced. All managers had to apply for the new roles — under interview conditions that were new, too.

The new structure was brought in on a region by region basis. The communication team had a limited involvement in the initial introduction in Glasgow. Feedback from this pilot region demonstrated that staff had a number of unresolved concerns — and that early, improved communication would have helped to alleviate these in advance of the new structure going live.

The Bank was quick to learn. Before the next phase of introduction — in Manchester — the communication team ran a series of focus groups to identify what staff wanted in terms of communication about the new structure. Based on the output of these, a series of communications was planned.

Local newsletters were introduced to give staff background information about the changes. These included timetables for the introduction and for the communication opportunities leading up to it. The newsletters had a strong customer focus — reflecting a key objective that the changes should be "invisible" to customers, with no interruption to quality of service. Help lines were also set up to answer staff queries.

Next, all staff were invited to an evening roadshow where the rationale for the change was explained. This comprised a presentation from the regional manager, followed by a question and answer session led by the regional manager and change team members, and facilitated by a local member of staff. Team leaders had gathered some questions beforehand, and fed broader issues into the Q and A session while responding to local queries themselves.

Videos were distributed to staff for viewing at home. These focused on the different jobs on offer, and on the selection process. Job fairs were next. These gave staff an opportunity to discuss each role on an individual basis. The people who designed each role explained how and where the job fitted the whole. Then someone who had actually started doing the job explained what it was really like in practice! An HR representative explained the selection process after which there was a panel discussion. Attendees then had the chance to talk on a one-to-one basis.

The final phase was to advertise the jobs and start the selection process in earnest. The emphasis on communication continued. Prior to the cutover when the new roles were introduced, the Bank ran a communication programme called "employees as ambassadors". This comprised a combination of video and role play, stressing the importance of effective interactions with customers.

Measurement was used at each stage of the programme. Questionnaires were distributed after every event. Focus groups were run to identify hot topics and to monitor the grapevine and respond.

Peter Casebow, internal communication manager, comments: "The communication programme made sure that staff were clear about the change underway. Not just the details of the jobs and the process, but also about timescales — what would happen when. This went a long way to dispelling uncertainty. We also made sure that questions were answered at the earliest stage. And the bottom line was that we were able to continue to run the business successfully with this huge change underway internally — but with customers continuing to get a high quality service."

- It is important to think through what staff could be feeling and thinking in advance of communicating major change. Encourage line managers who will be handling the announcement to do the same. A checklist of questions for managers to use when thinking through their communication to staff could include:
    — will I still have a job?
    — what will this mean to me?
    — how is this going to affect my area?

— how much sense does this make for the business?
People relate to change by thinking about the impact on themselves.
Think the communication through from this perspective.

- Plan the detail of communicating the change. What has to happen and by when? Make sure there is a logical sequence in place, and that people know their responsibilities. Draw up a detailed timetable. This is particularly important prior to an announcement where one area of the business will be affected by the change and needs to be briefed first. Work backwards from "D-day" and think through each stage. "Prompt" the key players to ensure that everything is on track.

- During major change, there may be long periods when there is nothing new to say. Don't allow a communication vacuum to develop or it will fill with rumour and speculation. Give regular updates. Let people know what process is taking place; why it is not possible to communicate anything new at this stage — and when they can expect firm decisions. Most importantly, use your feedback channels to monitor rumours and respond to them quickly.

- One communication manager reported that the timing of a key change project was kept on track primarily because the date when the announcement was to be made had been announced to staff in advance. This proved to be a valuable tool in keeping sufficient momentum behind the planning process, so preventing a long delay in communicating from causing additional anxiety in the workforce.

- To be effective, and to provide the change team with all the support they will need — briefing packs, questions and answers, etc, you will need early access to all information. Going about the planning task in a structured and logical way will enable you to demonstrate why this is necessary.

- Where the date for a major announcement is fixed in advance, some organisations have found it useful to build in time for a rehearsal a few days before the event. Involving the senior managers who will communicate on the day reassures them — and allows time for fine-tuning. This needs to be weighed against potentially increasing the time between a decision and its announcement — so increasing the potential for the grapevine to distort it.

- Sometimes change is more evolutionary. Changing the culture of an organisation is a long term process — and requires understanding of the need for change to succeed. A number of case studies in this document illustrate how change can be achieved by involving people throughout the organisation in a systematic way. Other solutions are more dramatic.

With cultural change, it is essential to get buy in as to why change is needed. The London Borough of Redbridge developed a radical way of freeing up discussion about deep seated communication and cultural issues. These included a long-standing tradition of secrecy and blame.

A cross-functional task force was set up to address communication as part of a radical review of the organisation. The group soon recognised that a communication strategy focusing on information flows, would not be enough to get people to confront the behavioural issues which were impeding success. The task force decided to focus on a communication strategy which addressed the issue of how to encourage people to recognise the need for a changed culture.

Their solution was dramatic. They commissioned a playwright to research what working for the council was like, and specifically the perception people had about communication. He interviewed a range of people from across the organisation — from the Chief Executive downwards. He then wrote a play based on his research. The plot focused on a new middle manager working in a fictional hierarchical organisation. She took the organisation's statements about innovation and initiative at face value and tried to change things. The play looked at how she fared.

Initially, staff were invited to attend the play in cross-functional groups, then break into discussion groups to look at the issues arising from the action. Subsequently, the play was re-run and work teams encouraged to attend together. Following the completion of the drama, the actors re-enacted scenes. The audience were divided into groups each with control over one actor, and could stop the action at any time to comment on what they felt would really happen. This use of forum theatre enabled employees working closely together to voice views and opinions through a third party, the actors, which may otherwise have continued to be bottled up, straining work relationships and affecting performance.

Paul Williams, Chair of the task group which conceived the idea comments: "The play was very useful in freeing up discussion about the issues that people face because of the behaviour of others — and the consequences of that. Attendance was on a voluntary basis, with approximately 1,500 of the 8,000 strong workforce attending. A number of teams have now chosen to examine those cultural issues more deeply and work on resolving them — because the awareness and ownership is firmly in place."

Planning for urgent news

- Though you are unlikely to know when a situation requiring urgent communication is likely to arise, you can be prepared for it.

- Make sure you are clear on the processes you will use to communicate urgent news and that everyone understands what they are before the need to use them arises. Most organisations use E-mail as the medium for getting news out fast. In places where not all staff have access to E-mail, additional systems need to be set up. These could include designating staff in each area as communication representatives, with responsibility for printing a hard copy of the E-mail and putting it on notice boards. Alternatively, managers could be given responsibility for cascading the news to their teams. Make sure people know the timescale they are expected to adhere to.

- If you are relying on individuals within the organisation to play an active role in communicating urgent news, make sure there is a robust system of deputies in place in case people are out when the news breaks. Give clear instructions about what needs to be communicated, to whom, and by when.

- If you have to rely on faxes to distribute copies of briefings, don't underestimate how long it takes to fax several pages of information to various locations. The frustration of knowing that a briefing session is due to start in ten minutes but that you physically cannot get the information to all the briefers in time is an experience no communication person should ever have to go through!

- If you need to act fast — be flexible. Providing notices to the receptionist or to security to hand to people as they leave work can be a good way of reaching everyone if news breaks close to the end of their day. And people will appreciate the effort you have made — particularly if they are likely to see or hear a reference to what has happened through the media.

Companies with their own business TV systems are able to communicate a consistent message to all employees very quickly. Digital used its in-house video network when a new chief executive was appointed in the UK.

The new incumbent was an unknown quantity. He was joining from outside Digital and, even more significantly, from a rival company which was perceived to have a very different corporate culture. Speculation abounded.

Within twenty-four hours of his appointment, he was in the video studio. The objective of the recording was to give a flavour of the man — to present him to as many people as possible, to reassure employees and reduce the amount of uninformed speculation — straight away. Within forty-eight hours of his appointment, the broadcast had been seen by fifty per cent of the employee population.

- Remember to follow up an urgent communication in the next regular team meeting or briefing. Encourage managers to use it as an opportunity to check that everyone has received and understood the information, or to give more detail as appropriate. Ask for questions and make sure they are answered.

Giving bad news

- Openness and honesty — to ensure the maximum levels of trust — are key factors when it comes to communicating bad news. Ensuring that line managers doing the communicating are equipped to manage the situation with maximum empathy is another vital ingredient.

- Managers need to be visible, supportive and available for their staff. They must listen and provide answers to questions where they can, and as quickly as they can. They need not be afraid to say they do not have the answer but that they will find out. This behaviour requires maturity and understanding. Think about the support your managers will require in advance of the bad news being announced, and put the necessary actions in place.

- Plan the communication of bad news from the perspective of the recipient.

- Make sure that the people directly affected know first — and that they are told face-to-face, so that they can ask questions and clarify their understanding. Having an effective communication plan, including a detailed timetable, is essential. Where people are personally affected; it may take time for the information to sink in, so provide additional opportunities for questions after the event.

- Ensure a robust feedback loop is in place, so that every question receives a response within the agreed timescale — even if the response is simply to explain why a full answer is not yet possible. Analysing the feedback to identify what the key issues are will help you as you go on to plan the next stage of the communication. Always make sure that staff concerns are responded to in the ongoing communication process.

- If the bad news is as a result of a business decision, make sure that people understand the rationale. Previous work ensuring consistent themes, locked into the company's business direction, should help here. One company described how a whole segment of the organisation was told that a decision had been made to integrate their work into other business streams. Their jobs were therefore redundant. This decision was in line with previous messages given by the organisation about the need to improve competitiveness and service. Though obviously sad at the decision, the team worked with real pride to ensure that the transfer of work was done in the most professional way — because they understood why the decision had to be taken.

The Body Shop faced bad news in the Summer of 1994 when a press feature making a series of allegations about the company was heavily hyped on both sides of the Atlantic for a fortnight before publication. This had serious implications externally and sent share prices tumbling. Internally, the situation was potentially just as serious. The Body Shop is founded on very strong values — and the allegations were throwing doubt on how real these were. The potential for loss of trust was immense.

Transparency is one of the key principles for The Body Shop. The company ensured that all press clippings reporting the allegations were made available to staff on a daily basis. This ensured that people were aware of the accusations that were being made. Then they rebutted what was being said. A combination of media was used. This included bringing managers together to brief them and respond to their questions, then providing them with briefing packs to use with their people. Staff could phone a hot line to hear a recording of what had been said and the response. Notices and cartoons were stuck on the backs of toilet doors! These helped simplify some of the complex issues under the microscope.

Prompt action, and communicating with people fairly and honestly ensured that respect for the company was maintained while the allegations were still in circulation. The actual article, once published, proved to be far less sensational than the press speculation had suggested and the share price rose again.

Keeping it consistent: actions and words

- A key role for the communication professional is to ensure that messages across the company are consistent — and that they can be seen in a broad context so that the rationale for whatever is being said or done is clear.

- One technique used by a number of companies is to have a process whereby all messages for company-wide distribution must be "cleared" through the communications unit. This allows an opportunity to check for consistency of message, tone, style etc.

- Abstracting key themes from the company's business strategy, and checking every communication against them for consistency, will ensure a minimum of communication "clutter".

- Consistency comes from action far more than words. Our beliefs are formed by what we see people doing rather than through what they say to us. Consistency between what a company says, and the behaviours it displays, is vital to build trust and avoid a loss of credibility. Everyone has seen the company where the values statement has been put up on the wall — and that's as far as it ever gets.

- Consistency in behaviour is far more likely if people have a sense of ownership for it and understand why it is important. Many companies use a workshop approach, bringing people together to look at the challenges ahead and what will be needed to address them. This gets "buy in" to the agreed behaviours.

> Lombard Personal Finance have six core messages. These are an articulation of the company's values. John Morgan, managing director,comments: "Communication is a lifetime pursuit that can so easily be put back in a company, for example by changes in people. The values are therefore most important. They are what provide consistency."
>
> The values were initially agreed by the Board, and disseminated through the company. Every action that the company takes comes from these six strands. The messages which have been developed from the values act as a yardstick against which all communication is tested for consistency.
>
> John comments "Success comes from using simple messages, and repeating them over and over, until everyone in the organisation can explain exactly what Lombard is all about. All our people should see themselves as stakeholders in the company. That means they have a right to know about the company, and how their job fits with the overall strategy. We need an agile company, with everyone sharing the success and the rewards, and understanding the need to change. You can't get that without looking at communication strategically.
>
> "Improving communication — so that the recipient sees it as having improved — is a ten year process. Managers need to overcome the old mindset that information is power. That means leadership from the top, demonstrating the importance of discussing issues with people regularly, and honestly. It means having formal communication processes, and ensuring that every business strategy has a communication plan built in. It means educating managers to understand the value of open communication. And it means being prepared to use management processes if people do not behave in accordance with the values."

- Most communication professionals interviewed for the book advised a softly softly approach to communicating values. It's important to avoid them becoming management speak — with people being sent a personal copy but nothing changing. Instead, the company needs to put effort into building the behaviours espoused in the values into the way it runs its business — its processes and its training.

> When Unipart was privatised in 1987, the new group of companies adopted a "stakeholder philosophy" as its set of core beliefs. The company set out to show how long-term, shared destiny relationships with its five key stakeholder audiences — customers, employees, shareholders, suppliers and communities in which the company does business — would provide a better business model for enduring success. The stakeholder philosophy suggests that in taking business decisions, the company should consider the impact on all stakeholders.

This has been demonstrated in actions as well as words. Employees enjoy a strong say in the running of the company through programmes like Our Contribution Counts Circles, a team building problem solving approach. They have their own 'university', the Unipart U, which promotes continuous learning in the workplace, an employee health and fitness centre called The Lean Machine, and an opportunity to have a financial share in the company through an employee share scheme.

In 1993, Unipart joined 25 other UK companies in a project launched by the Royal Society for the Arts. The RSA Tomorrow's Company Inquiry set out to study how UK businesses could compete in the new global marketplace. The results, published after two years of intense study and debate, stated that businesses will have greater opportunities for success if they can demonstrate an "inclusive approach" in which the needs of all stakeholders are considered and acted upon.

Initially, Unipart celebrated the publication through briefing meetings, supported by a special documentary produced as part of the company's in-house news video programme. Then, six months later, the company was given a unique opportunity to demonstrate how the stakeholder philosophy had been put into action. His Royal Highness, the Duke of Edinburgh, who is president of the RSA, asked to visit the company, to see how Unipart could demonstrate its beliefs in a stakeholder approach.

Rather than inviting His Royal Highness to a select meeting of senior managers, the company staged an event called Unipart Expo. This spanned nearly every aspect of Unipart's business, with audiences from all its stakeholder groups involved. The concept was to take His Royal Highness on tour through the Tomorrow's Company report, and illustrate it with real people who had done extraordinary things. This tour included presentations, an employee "birthday party", a tented village of stands hosted by community organisations, and a barbecue lunch for 2,000 people.

The aim of the event was to communicate some very complex ideas about trust and long term relationships with employees and other stakeholders — by showing how ideas had been put into action. In addition to involving the maximum number of staff in the event, a four page publication was distributed the following day. This was followed by a special documentary edition of the company, video, Grapevine, entitled "Ideas into Action".

Frank Nigriello, Group communications director for Unipart, comments: "Unipart Expo taught us a great deal about communicating complex subjects to a large number of people. I can't imagine that anyone could have left the event without being impressed by the power of the stakeholder philosophy and the spirit which people at all levels in the company have demonstrated in turning these ideas into a reality."

- Where managers are assessed against competencies, the appraisal process should reinforce the required behaviours. Monitoring mechanisms — such as feedback systems and company audits — can pinpoint any widespread issues and allow an analysis of why inconsistency is occurring.

> Celebrate success where people are making progress towards living the company's values. Cellnet has a communication programme in place to remind staff of what they are doing to make the values live. Avenues for doing this include displays, news sheets, and opportunities for staff to share what they have achieved with directors. Other activities have included a charity ball and a family "away day" at a theme park. A people panel made up of key players from around the business provides a sounding board for new ideas and initiatives. A "quality of working life" survey monitors progress.

- Context is as important as consistency. When a group of people has been immersed in a project, it is easy to forget that others do not have the same level of understanding. One of the roles of the communication professional is to help build bridges and make links. This may be through representing the other staff to the team — asking the questions that others would ask — to demonstrate the need to give the wider picture. Or it may be through using communication media to show the links between what is happening in the outside world and the company's strategies and actions.

Documents in this section

DOCUMENT No: 3.1	Description	Extract from communication strategy for the newly merged operating company, part of the Glaxo Wellcome Group (p1)
Organisation Glaxo Wellcome Operations		
Document Communication strategy		

A strategy for communicating within Glaxo Wellcome Operations

"Communication problem in the White House? No one told me we've got a communication problem"

Ronald Reagan

"Communication is not made without inconvenience even from worse to better".

Samuel Johnson.

1 Introduction: Why do we need a strategy ?

* There is a need for fundamental change within Glaxo Wellcome Operations
    - to achieve our stretching goals and become the supplier of choice.

*Internal communication is the vanguard of change
    - creating desire to change by communicating imperative for change and vision for the future.
    - building understanding of our strategies for change through communicating our improvement programme and progress against them.
    - encouraging shared ownership of change and of success by seeking, listening and acting on views, suggestions and ideas.
    - providing "early warning system" for rooting out problems before they become major issues.
    - ensuring understanding of individual-team contribution – what does it mean for me/us?
*Effective, efficient, communications process, and consistency of message, are vital to achieving change.

DOCUMENT No: 3.1
Organisation   Glaxo Wellcome Operations

Document   Communication strategy (p2)

Challenges in Defining a Strategy

Glaxo Wellcome Operations is made up of seven sites from four different backgrounds. The different locations therefore have differing cultures, levels of awareness and understanding, and approaches to communications.

The key challenge in defining a communications strategy is to achieve an appropriate balance between harmonising and consistency of approach on the one hand, with sufficient flexibility to retain local ownership for communications and meet varying needs on the other. A balance must also be achieved between top down and bottom up communications. The aim must be to get this balance right in order to empower people, through their clarity of understanding, to contribute their maximum potential towards becoming the supplier of choice.

The strategy therefore details:-

- our communications vision and communication principles: the future state to which we aspire.
- Where we are now.
- Our improvement priorities: the breakthroughs required during 1996 to move us towards our vision.
- Our main communication mechanisms and plans to move towards harmonisation and best practice without losing local ownership.
- The implementation and review process which will be used to steer these changes.
- The process to be used for defining communication plans which will be reflecting different levels of awareness/local needs of different locations.
- The standard measures and monitoring mechanisms to be used.

The proposals which follow take into account both the disciplines required for European Foundation for Quality Management (EFQM) and the requirements to meet communication standards to achieve Investors in People standards.

2   Vision

To help create a positive responsive environment where people are enabled to contribute their maximum potential towards Glaxo Wellcome Operations becoming the supplier of choice.

What will this look like ?

- Shared understanding of:

      - Business environment

      - Company's strategies

         i) Glaxo Wellcome Operations

         ii) Glaxo Wellcome plc

         iii) Commercial areas

      - Plans and goals

      - Roles of different areas

      - Team contribution

      - Personal contribution

- Understanding and acceptance of why change is needed and vision for the future

       ↓

- Understanding of changing customer requirements/dedication to meeting them

- Willingness to change own behaviour at every level within organisation.

eg: Creating open, honest culture

            Welcoming ideas and contribution

            Encouraging challenges

            Taking challenges on board

- Environment that encourages openness even where there is little security

      - Teamwork/Sharing

      - Best practice

- Staff who are ambassadors to wider community -

      - ie: wider Glaxo Wellcome world

      - local environment/community

-Behavioural implications: Utilising and building on strengths

       Trust

       Mutual support

       Common goals

DOCUMENTS

DOCUMENTS

DOCUMENT No: 3.1
Organisation Glaxo Wellcome Operations

Document   Communication strategy (p4)

3   Communication Principles

Principle	What this will look like

Responsibility	- Every manager has commitment to/ ownership of communications
	- Staff feel and are empowered (links to acting on feedback)
	- Staff have tools which empower them
	    - through personal development
	    - through continuous improvement tools

Timeliness	- Early communication of decisions - Give timetables for decision taking - Monitor grapevine - respond promptly
Openness	- Maximum openness and honesty - Policy on confidentiality
360° Communications Boss Peers —— Customers/ Suppliers Staff	- Listening valued as highly as giving information - Listening followed by action/response - Links demonstrated between feedback/ decisions/actions - Feedback loops for every formal communications channel - Feedback used to ensure knowledge / views of whole organisation can be captured and used to strengthen future plans / activities
Relevance/ Accuracy	- All communications support business objectives - Consistency of messages with behaviours and activities - Information interpreted at every level to ensure it is meaningful to recipient - Fullness of information: checks for understanding/all questions answered - Reasons explained - Communications are simple/clear

4   Company Overview: Our Routemap

FROM	TO
Communications largely downwards/ concerns that feedback is ignored .	Two way listening with <u>action</u> to improve business performance. Feedback built into business planning mechanism.
High level of monitoring required/patchy commitment to communications by managers.	All managers regard communications as fundamental to their role and have necessary skills
Lack of systematic measures/ company-wide monitoring/review processes.	Measures, monitoring and review processes in place.
Interventionist communications processes.	Integrated communications process
Inconsistency between messages and behaviour.	All actions consistent with key messages communicated.
Barriers to understanding between teams/poor lateral communications.	Strong 360° communications facilitating partnership.
Challenge filtered out/not acted on.	Challenge encouraged and welcomed
Isolated pockets of excellence.	Best practice sought out and implemented across company - where implementation will improve business performance. External bench marking.

DOCUMENT No: 3.2

Organisation BT
Document Corporate Employee Communication
Plan 1994/95

Description Extract from annual corporate
employee communication plan (p1)

Corporate Employee Communications Plan 1994/95

Corporate Employee Communications Plan 1994/95

1 Employee communications programme objectives

Background

1993/94 has been an interesting - in many ways momentous - year for telecommunications around the world. Twelve months ago, we said the main task for employee communications would be combating low morale, but we have been helped by a number of events and activities. Our deal with MCI, the launch of (NewCo), progress in Europe and the Pacific Rim, the start of Breakout, a number of exciting pricing announcements, an increased focus on sales and marketing, more aggressive advertising and our Chairman's knighthood, combined with consistent net positive press coverage and strong financial performance, have done much to engender a feeling that something positive is happening. A key task is to build on this and capture what seems to be the beginning of renewed optimism.

That said, there are a number of factors that could nip nascent optimism in the bud. The 1994 employee attitude (CARE) survey shows that job security, career development and dissatisfaction with pay and benefits continue to be major issues. People remain negative about the benefits of change for BT employees and feel there is room to improve further our internal communications, particularly the timeliness and flow of information about the company's future direction, business performance and technological developments.

CARE does, however, show significant improvements in our customer focus and management behaviour and confirms a growing belief that BT will become the most successful worldwide telecommunications group. This belief will be tested in a tough year with the unions as we pursue a further 15,000 job losses in 1994/95 and seek to control our ongoing paybill costs. People are still seeking reassurances of a kind that cannot be given about future prospects and job security. They are also increasingly concerned about growing bureaucracy. The need for clear and honest communications with employees and their representatives has never been greater.

Key objectives for 1994/95

In 1994/95 we must build on positive achievement. This is the year we should hammer home the message that BT people are part of a global company. Now we have established the US connection with the MCI deal, made progress in Europe, started to establish ourselves in the Pacific Rim and reshaped to focus on global activities, a key communications objective will be to work towards creating a global culture within BT by building awareness internally of BT's growing international presence.

We will also communicate the importance of Breakout - concentrating not just on *what* is happening, but on *why*. We must build commitment and a sense of excitement, aiming to gain buy-in from all stakeholders and to ensure the achievements and philosophy of Breakout become part of business as usual for all BT people. There is already widespread interest and demand for information - and a danger of misinterpretation, as some people remain convinced it is primarily a downsizing exercise. Our objective will be to position it firmly as the programme that will enable BT to win, to generate revenue both at home and abroad, and as something involving everyone. Communicating the importance of revenue generation is key.

Issue: 1
Date: April 1994

Corporate Employee Communications Plan 1994/95

Finally, we must explain how the apparently negative fits with the positive, always considering the people implications of our communications. For some time, we have worked hard to communicate messages associated with the commercial imperative. This year, with a background of sustained growth in demand, a focus on sales and marketing through the Winning Matters programme and the positive issues associated with Breakout and global achievements, it is even more important to be specific about why there is *still* a need to downsize and why the commercial imperative *remains* important. These are hard people messages, and timeliness and consistency are key issues. Our objective will be to ensure all communications plans for all major company-wide activity and announcements not only demonstrate that the people implications of the messages have been considered, but also illustrate clearly the link to our key themes: "Winning Matters" and "Shaping up to Win" (see section 3, below). If a project or message does *not* link, we should ask how we can reshape it and, if we cannot, if we should be doing or communicating it at all.

2 *Key company-wide themes and supporting activity*

Last year, the aim of employee communications was to build commercial awareness, heighten understanding of the need for change and combat low morale by encouraging BT people to focus on the customer. These issues are all still high on the agenda, so "Winning Matters" remains a potent theme for 1994/95.

However, it no longer encompasses *everything* we need to communicate. Breakout has started, and we must convey the image of a powerful, growing organisation that is building on past success, knows where it is going, is firmly focused on delighting the customer and is taking the actions necessary to beat the competition by reshaping itself and *moving forward as a united team* to meet future challenges. These messages can all be integrated under the Breakout umbrella using the banner "Shaping up to Win".

Together "Winning Matters" and "Shaping up to Win" encapsulate our commitment to invest in the future, win new business and generate revenue - and to succeed. They will be supported by specific employee communications activity.

Winning Matters

The task is to reinforce the significance of competition and regulation in a new and refreshing way, reinforcing the relevance of the commercial imperative at *local* and *individual* level. The emphasis will be on beating the competition through service excellence. Communications will keep people aware of competitor activity and BT's response, and provide ammunition so BT people can act as ambassadors and sell more. There will be continuing emphasis on the value for money and service quality BT offers.

To support this awareness of competitor activity, a major face-to-face event for all PCGs is planned for April 1994. There will also be a follow up to the Winning Matters campaign. Several other enabler campaigns will be undertaken through the year, including campaigns to improve financial awareness, to ensure all BT people understand the company's strategy, to show how overseas investments and alliances help build towards the vision and to promote BT's importance to the UK economy and its progress towards the EQA.

Shaping up to Win

We will build on the past successes of TQM, Putting Customers First, Project Sovereign, the Leadership Programme and Involving Everyone, positioning Breakout as the programme which will deliver radical improvement, enabling BT to win. We will communicate the message that change is driven by customer needs and is not capricious. By demonstrating past and present success, we will show that change is about beating the competition (as opposed to downsizing) and that BT can and will win.

Issue: 1
Date: April 1994

DOCUMENT No: 3.2	Organisation Document	BT Corporate Employee Communication Plan 1994/95 (p3)

Corporate Employee Communications Plan 1994/95

We must mobilise BT people by communicating the idea of a virtuous circle; by delighting the customer and getting involved in Breakout, BT people will together improve BT's prospects and reputation, making it a better company to work for and to be associated with. We will also drive home the message that BT is serious about empowering its people and about cutting bureaucracy.

A separate communications plan for Breakout has been prepared by the project team in conjunction with CRD, so that it dovetails with other corporate activities and campaigns. Recognising the need for careful planning and cohesion between communicating the positive messages associated with Breakout and other negative messages, close liaison between the Breakout team and CRD, will be maintained throughout the project's lifetime. In addition, monitoring and sign-off of all divisional and unit communications concerning Breakout will be undertaken by the CRD/Breakout communications team.

3 *Measurement and targets*

This year, the overall success of company-wide communications will be measured in two main ways - by the response to selected communications-related questions in the annual CARE survey and by CRD's Omnibus surveys. The first gives a general company-wide overview of employee attitude towards key aspects of employee communications policy and practice; the second allows more detailed analysis as the year goes on, of specific channel performance and message recall and understanding.

CARE survey

A detailed review of the 1993/94 Corporate Employee Communications Plan, including a full review of latest CARE results against company-wide targets, will be prepared at the end of the financial year. Meanwhile, company-wide employee communications targets for the next CARE survey, based on 1993/94 results for selected benchmark questions, have been set as follows:

Q	Measure	1993/4% result	1995% target
6.1	Fully/fairly well informed	55	58
6.3a	Agree information provided is honest	33	43
6.3b	Agree information provided is relevant	33	43
6.3c	Agree information provided is understandable	41	46
6.3d	Agree information provided arrives on time	20	30
5.4b	Team meetings useful source of information	62	65
6.4	Employee communications better	27	37
6.5	Confident my manager communicates openly	61	64
6.7	Confident my views communicated upwards	46	51

(Divisional/unit targets should be set by reference to the following formula: if performance, as measured by the last CARE survey, is lower than 40%, a 10% improvement should be sought; if performance is between 40% and 50%, a 5% improvement; and if performance is over 50%, a 3% improvement.)

Omnibus surveys

Omnibus surveys aim to investigate the success of selected communications initiatives on a company-wide basis by checking awareness of campaigns and recall/understanding of key messages.

Issue: 1
Date: April 1994

Corporate Employee Communications Plan 1994/95

Research is conducted by an independent market research company in one-to-one interviews with representative samples of BT people. Omnibus surveys are run approximately every ten weeks, but their scheduling is deliberately flexible to meet the needs of the business. The selection of research topics is done on a relatively short timescale for the same reason. (It is worth noting that Omnibus surveys are conducted by CRD *in addition to* measurement of individual channel performance, such as readership surveys for corporate publications and audience research for broadcast media.)

The Omnibus format was trialled early in 1993 and, so far, three surveys have been conducted. As we are still at the data-gathering stage, it would be inappropriate to set specific performance targets until clear patterns begin to emerge. During the first half of 1994/95, however, CRD, in conjunction with BT's Management Sciences Consultancy Unit (MSCU), will monitor results with the aim of setting minimum percentage targets, relating to awareness and accuracy of recall.

Our aim is to recognise patterns that will allow realistic anticipation of a certain level of awareness and recall/understanding relating to channel used, eg a piece of direct mail should produce a higher level of awareness than an article in *BT today*, and we can and should set higher percentage targets for both awareness and understanding. In this way, we can begin to build specific Omnibus-related targets into campaign communications plans, balancing channel costs against the needs of the business.

Work on trends and target setting relating to Omnibus is already underway. Further details will be issued during 1994/95 and CRD will aim to set definite targets by 1 October 1994.

4 *Looking to the future*

The needs of the business and its people are changing. Over the next five years, new ways of communicating will be called for and issues of policy, control, access and response will need to be rethought. This section looks ahead to what issues may emerge and is intended as a starting point for discussion.

Working from home

Teleworking will be a key issue for employee communications over the next five years. By the year 2000, a far larger proportion of people will be working from home; certainly, the number based routinely in BT buildings will decrease. People's jobs are becoming increasingly based outside the traditional office and we need to recognise this and allow for it in our communications strategy. It is happening with our field engineers already and, increasingly, it will apply to others, including more and more managers and professionals. Our aim must be to communicate with BT people who use home or an alternative location as a workplace as efficiently as if they were working in a BT building. This may require a radical rethink of existing policies and channels.

BT Business Television

Business TV has developed rapidly as a communications channel in the two years since its inception. Our current aim is to roll-out to PCGs by March 1994 and we will now be considering whether to submit a business case to include all MPGs within the following year. There is also the issue of how Business TV can be exploited fully. It will never be a line instrument, but it could be a powerful functional communications tool. Already we are thinking about broadcasting specialist programmes for specific audiences (such as our retail sales force) via the Business TV network, and this needs to be developed into a definite policy.

Issue: 1
Date: April 1994

DOCUMENT No: 3.2

Organisation Document

BT Corporate Employee Communication Plan 1994/95 (p5)

Corporate Employee Communications Plan 1994/95

Meanwhile, the use of screens to communicate real-time information to our people could allow development of a teletext service, currently available in BT Centre as Newscreen, via the Business TV network. Ideally, over the next five years, we should move to a national system, linked to all BT buildings.

Electronic mail

The development of e-mail will be critical over the coming five years. There are two aspects. One is simple messaging - once all BT people have access to a screen capable of sending information and of receiving messages from a central source, the task of corporate and, by extension, divisional communications will be greatly facilitated. One of our greatest problems - people hearing news about BT externally before they hear it from the company - will, in large measure, be solved. Clear guidelines on acceptable use will need to be developed to avoid misuse - we must, for example, limit unsupervised mass mailings and place access controls on senior managers' mailboxes - but between now and the end of the millennium we should move towards the ideal of universal network access.

The second issue is related, but requires greater organisation and a change in the way we work. Increasingly, we should aim to hold on a central database many documents and directories we currently publish and distribute at great cost to the business. Their life-span is limited (they are often out of date before they reach their audience) and distribution systems are over-burdened. Ideally, BT should store documents like its annual report to shareholders, directories, *1001 facts*, ISIS documents, sales and marketing literature, briefings, press releases and even the daily news cuttings on a central database capable of being accessed by an internal audience. We could start with a limited audience, moving to the ideal solution where everyone in BT can access what he or she needs. Access to communications must ultimately be demand-driven with the customer in control.

Multimedia

Given that there are between 60,000 and 70,000 personal computers in BT, pc-based multimedia packages will have an important role in employee communications within five years. The ability to store data in a variety of forms - text, photograph, illustrations, voice, video etc - and to enable the user to interact with this information, makes possible a communications revolution. CRD is currently working on the design specification of multimedia packages and commissioning developmental work. Within a year, for example, it ought to be possible to equip senior managers - particularly those in the sales community - with a multimedia BT presentation pack that could be run on a pc anywhere in the world.

Publications

There remain publications whose purpose is unclear and new publications are beginning to spring up. We should review again the total BT portfolio, seek to streamline it, identify and reduce costs and look again at improving the design and content of those publications that remain. We must stop duplication of material and encourage a greater use of recycled and/or environmentally friendly products.

Issue: 1
Date: April 1994

DOCUMENT No: 3.2	Document	Corporate Employee Communication Plan 1994/95 (p6)
Organisation BT		

Corporate Employee Communications Plan 1994/95

Face-to-face communications

We should commit to face-to-face communications as a major channel over the next five years, although, as time goes on, this will become more difficult to manage. But we should nevertheless aim for an improvement in the short to medium term, pushing corporate CARE targets for team meetings towards 100%. Additionally, we need to improve the *quality* of face-to-face interactions. In many parts of BT, there has been no real attention paid to this for a long time and, like any system, team meetings are suffering because of lack of maintenance and update. In 1994/95, we suggest research is done to find out if first-line managers need specific refresher training.

Global communications

BT is fast developing into a multi-national and, therefore, multi-cultural and multi-lingual company. Over the next five years, an increasing number of people will be based outside the UK and, as a result, a number of communications issues will need to be addressed. It may no longer be appropriate for key internal documents to be published only in English. Similarly, we must recognise that most corporate communication channels are currently shaped by UK culture and aimed at a UK audience; for this reason, they may not have the same level of effectiveness outside this country. The distances involved place special constraints on existing channels, and these will increasingly need to be tailored to suit overseas requirements. Team meetings, for example, involving BT people overseas and people in wholly or partly owned subsidiaries, will need to be developed and managed carefully, recognising that cultural differences may reduce their effectiveness in some places. Finally, inter-regional communications will become increasingly important, to encourage the sharing of best practice in the communication of non-UK orientated business activities.

Process improvement

CRD is already addressing process improvement on a company-wide basis through its *Communicate with BT People* project. Over the next five years we would look to continue to take the lead in coordinating company-wide channel development and process improvement work across all Divisions.

Issue: 1
Date: April 1994

DOCUMENT No: 3.2	Organisation	BT
	Document	Corporate Employee Communication Plan 1994/95 (p7)

Corporate Employee Communications Plan 1994/95

5   Corporate Employee Communications issues 1994/95

	A	M	J	J	A	S	O	N	D	J	F	M	Note
AGM - pre-AGM employee evening													1
APR/PDR: for ETGs													2
APR/PDR: for MPGs													2
APR/PDR: for non-managers (x ETGs)													2
APR/PDR: for PCGs													2
BREAKOUT													
BT Quality Awards													
Business travel													
CARE survey/CARE action planning													
Chairman's Conference													
Competition/regulation													
Corporate clothing													
Corporate communications plan/EC plan													
Corporate strategy review 1994													
Environmental Performance Report 1994													
EQA self-assessment													
Financial results													
Innovation 94													3
Marketing programmes	?	?	?	?	?	?	?	?	?	?	?	?	4
MCI/NewCo													
New Ideas													
Non-management development													
Pay: MPG													
Pay: NCU, UCW and CMA						?	?	?					
Pay: PCG													
PCG Roadshow													5
Poor performance/attendance													
Pricing issues													
Quality of Service statistics													
Release 94													
Sales/product launches	?	?	?	?	?	?	?	?	?	?	?	?	4
Winning Matters													
Workstyle 2000/Workstyle 94													

Key: CRD/EC priorities at 3/94, based on current information

░	EC activity
▓	High level of EC activity

Notes:

1 Pre-AGM Employee Evening 1994 is on 27 July at Wembley, London

2 Annual Performance Review/Performance Development Review

3 Innovation 94 will take place at Martlesham - for customers and selected PCGs

4 No details at this stage - but this calendar will be regularly reviewed and reissued

5 Roadshow dates 14-21 April (in 7 venues across the UK)

Issue: 1
Date: April 1994

DOCUMENT No: 3.3 Organisation Lombard Personal Finance	Document Description	Communication Strategy Extract from internal communications strategy demonstrating links between business and and communication objective (p1)

The role of communications

There are six strands to the sector strategy:

- Customer care
- Empowerment
- Market 2000
- Information
- IT harnessed to business needs
- European integration

Our sector vision is: *to be market leader in personal finance sourced through third party partners and direct, in chosen European markets, providing quality service and value to these customers, while offering competitive value to the end user.*

Effective communication can reinforce the strategic direction and place information received by staff within a solid framework. The core ethos and values of the organisation are integral to determining the messages to communicate. At Sector we are empowered, European and reward innovation and endeavour. We believe in treating everyone as a partner in the business, with open, honest and timely communication.

These strategies and values will only be believed if actions support them. All the bulletins, conferences etc will not get buy in if the belief in them from our leaders is not genuine and actions are not shaped by them at the most senior level.

3

DOCUMENTS

DOCUMENT No: 3.3
Organisation   Lombard Personal Finance

Document   Communication Strategy (p2)

Communication Objectives

A communications strategy is a support strategy, specifically designed to support business objectives. Our communications objectives therefore emanate from the business issues established within the Balanced Business Scorecard:

- **Long term sustainable growth**
- **Commitment to outstanding performance**
- **Operational Excellence**
- **Outstanding value for customers**

To convert these into communication objectives:

Business Objective:
Long term sustainable growth

Communications Objective:
All staff know the on-going profitability and performance of the sector, against established targets

Measurable aims:
- *All staff know that the continued profitability of our business is critical*
- *All staff know our goal of £100m trading performance by year 2000*
- *All staff know the half yearly and annual results from a sector perspective*
- *In relevant departments, staff know their monthly new business targets and how they are performing against target*
- *Each quarter all staff know how we are performing against target as a sector*

4

DOCUMENT No: 3.3

Organisation	Lombard Personal Finance
Document	Communication Strategy (p3)

Business Objective:
Commitment to outstanding performance

Communications Objective:
Staff partnership in business: all staff provided with all the information and knowledge they need to make this business successful

Measurable aims:

- *All staff have all the information they need to perform outstandingly*
- *Feedback mechanisms are actively used by all staff to feed information upwards and horizontally*
- *Information fed upwards is actively used and its use reported to maintain the cycle*
- *Immediacy and urgency is given to 'need to know' market and product information for all staff*
- *Regularly measure staff attitudes and perceptions*
- *Senior management accessible and approachable to all staff and buy in actively to the communications process*

Business Objective:
Operational Excellence

Communications Objective:

Quality and efficiency essential to our success

Measurable aims:

- *Our long term productivity management vital to our profitability*
- *Continual assessment of "best practice' and most effective ways of processing business essential*
- *Quality is essential part of everything we do*
- *Understanding the need for responsible lending and effective credit scoring*

5

DOCUMENT No: 3.3

Organisation   Lombard Personal Finance

Document   Communication Strategy (p4)

Business Objective:

Outstanding value for customers

Communications Objective:

Excellent levels of customer satisfaction of prime importance; quality customer service keeps us competitive

Measurable aims:

- *All staff aware of the prime importance of quality customer service*

- *We have the highest ethical standards and comply with all regulations by which we are bound*

- *All staff aware of the legislation governing our business and its importance (ie money laundering)*

1   Business transformation:

Business Objective:
Commitment to outstanding performance

Communications Objective:
Business transformation - An environment of continual change and improvement

For a specific change project, the communications objectives would depend on the business objectives of that project.

Neglect of the human dimension when planning and implementing business process reengineering or business transformation is a major contributor to failure. It is essential to make people receptive to change - "defrosting" them, by developing a programme of activity designed to advise and explain the need for change, the benefits change will bring to them as well as to the business. Focusing on changing the culture and the attitudes of staff and developing their skills so that they are competent and confident to work within the organisation as it changes is fundamental to success.

DOCUMENT No: 3.3 Organisation Document Lombard Personal Finance Communication Strategy (p5)

For a specific change project, the communications objectives would depend on the business objective of that project. However, as a general principle, one should not just report conclusions, one should take people through the thought process. Once objectives are clear, communication can begin. The cycle should be as follows;

Establish the framework

Key why messages
Awareness of company values and objectives
Know the proposition

Assess current reality

Staff attitudes
Leadership skills available?
Purpose/positioning

Set communications strategy

Communications KEY enabler
Methodologies for delivering message

Implement, evaluate, learn

Reinforce decision, linking back to key why messages
Benefits
Feedback loop
Thanks

7

DOCUMENTS

DOCUMENT No: 3.3

Organisation Lombard Personal Finance

Document Extract from communication action plan showing how strategy is converted to action (p1)

DOCUMENTS

Business Objective: *Operational Excellence*

Communications Objective: *Staff partnership in the business: all staff provided with the information and knowledge they need to make this business successful*

Activity	Milestone	Performance against milestone
Audit of current business unit needs and activities	Q3 95 - initial audit undertaken Q1 96 - Further research to be done	Dedicated communications manager to be appointed Lombard Bank.
Sector Conference		Two planning meetings have now taken place. Creatives to be presented 4th June.
Team meetings and briefings	Q1 96 - part of research into current activity - skills testing may be required	Feedback awaited from team meeting training undertaken in Banking Services. Weekly briefing sheet available to team meeting organisers on request.
Staff attitude surveys	Group survey Q4 95	Results now available. Business unit action plans ongoing. Results announced in Bulletin. To be discussed at next forum.
Corporate behaviour assessment	Not required at this stage	
Communication Forums	Quarterly	Q1 96 forum to be held on 21st March in Enfield. Holland forum to take place Q2.

3

96

DOCUMENT No: 3.3

Organisation Document — Lombard Personal Finance Communication action plan (p2)

Business Objective: *Commitment to outstanding performance*

Communications Objective: *Business transformation: Environment of continual change and improvement*

Activity	Milestone	Performance against milestone
Corporate identity launch	Q4 95 launch to staff	Project ongoing. LTF to agree their involvement. Roll out on course.
Vision and mission statement review - in a language the audience can understand	Q1 96	New Sector review on vision and mission in line with the implementation of EQM.
Personal development programmes to encourage the right attitude	Q2 96: launch opportunities to all staff	To be discussed further with forum members.
Sector Board include 'Communications' on agenda against business objectives	Comms issues to be brought forward for JMM's awareness prior to Sector Board.	All communication representatives to notify SJF of relevant issues.

DOCUMENTS

DOCUMENT No: 3.3
Organisation Lombard Personal Finance

Document   Lombard Personal Finance
Communication action plan (p3)

Business Objective: *Operational Excellence*

Communications Objective: *Staff partnership in the business: all staff provided with the information and knowledge they need to make this business successful*

Activity	Milestone	Performance against milestone
Interactive Multimedia PCs in each location	Q1 96. Content & production to be agreed.	Terms of reference drafted. Supplier and IT requirements currently being determined. Consultant shortlisted.
Sector Bulletin	Bi-monthly production	Bulletin 3/96 due in June. Topics to be advised.
Monthly E-mail to Heads of Dept across Sector updating Group/Nat West market/product information and 'Views from the Top'	To commence Q1 96	Three reports have now been circulated via E-mail to senior management team. No feedback at this stage.
Intranet	Q1 96	Internal net currently available on Axis compatible machines, but not in Personal Sector. SJF taking up with sector IT. Opportunities of Intranet to be discussed at next group meeting.

4

DOCUMENT No: 3.4

Organisation   Bass Taverns
Document   Employee Communications Policy

Description   Employee communication policy summarising the company's philosophy and methods (p1).

BASS TAVERNS

EMPLOYEE COMMUNICATIONS POLICY

POLICY:

Bass Taverns believes that communicating with its employees and involving them through feedback is essential if the company is to help employees meet their aspirations, strengthen company performance and secure the long term success of the business.

Employee communications are a principle line management responsibility. Open and effective two-way communications between managers and their staff are seen as key, and Taverns will ensure that its management receive training in the necessary skills and core competencies to ensure this.

The key to communicating with all employees will be through regular team meetings with their immediate line managers, supported by a comprehensive communications programme which will ensure that:

- Employees are kept fully informed about decisions and developments that are likely to affect Bass Taverns, their jobs, working environment, prospects, immediate work group or unit.

- Employees are kept fully informed about the company's priorities and its objectives, along with the activities of the rest of the Bass Group.

- Employees have their views — on matters which affect them or where their experience enables them to make a valued contribution — recognised and utilised as part of the decision-making and/or implementation process.

PRACTICE:

The policy will be achieved through using a mixture of the different media/processes set out below, with the key route being the Team Meeting that a line manager holds with his/her team.

The best method for getting specific messages across will always be that which takes into account all viewpoints and the different classifications of staff being addressed.

METHODS:

This section gives a brief overview of the media/processes that can be used within Bass Taverns for communicating with employees.

1. Team Meetings

Surveys continue to show that most people still prefer face-to-face communication, preferably from their immediate line manager, as it generates a sense of involvement and belonging. It also

DOCUMENT No: 3.4
Organisation Bass Taverns

Document   Employee Communication Policy
(p2)

provides the opportunity for checking individuals' understanding of the messages given and encourages two-way communication and feedback.

Successful team meetings are regular, relevant, run by the team leader and monitored.

The meeting should concentrate on the operational needs of the particular team and allow time for an element of "briefing down" of the core Bass Taverns messages.

Information presented should be relevant, with about 60% of it having a local bias, falling typically into one of the four categories:

* progress and performance
* policy
* people
* points for action

This meeting should, ideally, be held on a regular four weekly basis, within 8 working days of the distribution of the Core Brief. (See item 2). It should be run by the line manager/team leader with meeting dates diaried well in advance and not changed except in emergency. Where geographical constraints reduce the frequency of the meetings it is the team leader's responsibility to ensure the timely delivery of information through alternative methods. (See below.)

It should include LHMs via their NRI Team Meetings, who must then cascade the information to their Retail Staff, either at separate briefings or at their regular SWC meetings.

Team leaders have the key role in managing the flow of feedback and upward communications through the management chain.

Regular monitoring of the team meeting system will help to ensure that it is running efficiently and achieving its aims.

2. Core Brief

This will be prepared centrally on a four weekly basis, within two working days of the Bass Taverns Board/Executive meeting. It will be distributed electronically to all Senior Management, so that they are able to start the Team Meeting cascade outlined above.

The Brief will contain key messages that must be communicated to everyone, and further information that Team Leaders can choose to brief or not, depending on its relevancy to their specific teams. Wherever possible a local flavour needs to be added to the material.

The document is not intended to be briefed verbatim, but used as an aide memoir so that it can be individualised by the manager giving the brief so that it suits his/her personal style.

3. Reviews

All managers will hold an Annual review with each of their members of staff, so that they can

DOCUMENT No: 3.4   Organisation   Bass Taverns
                      Document   Employee Communication Policy
                                                 (p3)

review individual performance and progress, which will have been backed up by quarterly reviews throughout the year.

4. Surveys

Any survey conducted will provide vital information about how the company is performing and whether or not it is meeting its targets. They establish benchmarks against which the company can see how it has progressed. The results can be used to help the board formulate its policies and strategy and improve the way everyone works to achieve the company's aims.

They are an opportunity for employees to voice how they feel about a wide range of subjects, including their jobs, terms and conditions, training and appraisals, their managers, customers, communications and the Company as a whole.

The Company will conduct an Annual Employee Survey each year, coordinated by the Employee Communications Manager.

There will be a bi-annual Communications Survey.

5. Focus Groups

These will be held as follow up to initial surveys to probe specific areas/topics more deeply or to obtain a cross spectrum of employee views on a specific one-off initiative, programme etc.

6. Recognition and Saying Thank-you!

Whilst the company operates formal awards schemes, recognition for good work and for emulating Taverns culture and values, it must not be left to these alone.

Everyone needs to feel valued in order to give of their best.

Saying thank-you shows people what is expected, what can be done, and helps to create a supportive working environment where people know that their best efforts will be recognised and feel part of the company. Failure to recognise when someone has done well can be one of the most demoralising and demotivating of work experiences. It is line management's responsibility to recognise success and effort within their teams.

7. Communicating Bad News

If Bass Taverns has to deliver bad news, or major organisational change, it will:

*   tell all employees what is happening as soon as possible
*   treat all employees with dignity
*   give as many details as possible
*   use line managers to deliver the messages wherever possible

DOCUMENTS

DOCUMENT No: 3.4	Document	Employee Communication Policy (p4)
Organisation Bass Taverns		

* If all the details are not available, tell employees when they will be available
* fully explain the commercial rationale of the changes/news
* ensure that everyone, however affected, respects the way decisions have been made and communicated

8. Written Communications to LHMs

All communications to LHMs to be by memo, unless it is a personal communication and a letter is appropriate. Any correspondence from the centre to follow this principle.

All Area offices will mail shot their LHMs on a weekly basis. The centre will also use this facility for sending out circulars, briefing notes, etc.

Where the centre send any correspondence/circulars to LHMs the information must be circulated in advance to Trade Management, so that they are pre-briefed.

9. Road Shows/Presentations

These will be held on an ad hoc basis across the company, as determined by the specific message that needs to be conveyed to employees.

10. Walking the Job

Walking the job is an opportunity for senior and line managers to build up regular contact with employees by setting aside time to visit the workplace to discuss, in an informal manner, individual and team achievements, ideas and problems.

It also provides the opportunity to get informal feedback on issues already communicated through other channels and to say thank-you to staff personally for work they have done.

11. Vacancy Notices

Regular publication of all internal vacancies up to Group Resource Level, along with Bass PLC Group Managerial vacancies.

This will be distributed via the Infrastructure Notice board, across all of Bass Taverns IT Networks.

12. National Magazine—Inn Touch

This will be published from the centre on a regular cycle, so that at least 6 copies are printed in the course of a year.

It will be used for:

* increasing employee understanding of the company and hence motivation

* creating a sense of belonging
* developing team spirit across the company
* carrying business information and increasing awareness of business strategy and issues
* increasing awareness of new products, branding and other marketing and PR issues

"Specials" will also be produced under this mechanism, to provide information on specific projects/initiatives and the Annual Results for Taverns and PLC.

13. News Letters

When produced these will be owned by the Area or the Function generating it eg I.T. News.

Area Newsletters, whilst owned by the Retail Directors, should be biased towards Retail Staff and focus on Customer Service and Staff recognition.

Any Functional news letters produced for LHMs must be approved by the Operations Committee or the Employee Communications Steering Committee.

They must be short — no more than 4 sides A4 — and use a minimum of colour.

14. Conferences

A National Company Conference at least every two years, organised by the centre.

Retail Directors will hold Area Conferences at their discretion, and their cost.

The Executive will hold Senior Managers Forums at least twice per annum.

15. LHMs Forums

Held quarterly in each Area involving the Retail Director, RMBs and representatives from the LHMs and NRI teams in that area.

The purpose of the meeting will be motivational and to discuss policy issues.

16. Standard Notice Boards

These are to be used for supporting key messages that confirm senior appointments (ie DR upwards) and formalise decisions taken by PLC and the Bass Taverns Board, plus any people messages relevant to employees in a specific notice board area.

Their use is intended to increase circulation for interest/general information only. Anything requiring 'action' should not be attached to boards.

Each board will be looked after by a nominated individual.

DOCUMENT No: 3.4
Organisation   Bass Taverns

Document   Employee Communication Policy
(p6)

Key briefing notes and appointments will be E-mailed direct to the 'Minders' for their immediate attention.

17. Infrastructure E-Mail

E-Mail will be used in preference to memos, the exception being where the recipient is not set up to receive E-mail or where it is necessary to have a signatured memo.

Ideally long attachments, copying a number of people, should not be sent by E-mail as it can significantly reduce the network's efficiency.

The Employee Communications Manager, with the assistance of the I.T. department, will maintain Circulation Lists for the Board, Senior Managers and Departmental Heads that can be accessed via E-mail, under the Global Address book facility.

18. Infrastructure Bridge

Used to display key messages or topical information, that can be changed on a weekly basis (minimum standard).

Any department can request, through the Employee Communication Manager, to book a specific week for a message.

As soon as PLC's Annual & Interim Results have been released to the Stock Exchange, they will be displayed on the Bridge.

19. Infrastructure Notice Board

In addition to the standard notice system there will be one maintained under Bass Taverns Infrastructure and which is accessible not only to office bound employees but to all mobile workers via their Laptops.

In addition to the information that can be found on the standard boards, it will also contain Competitor information, up-to-date vacancies, manuals and standard documentation.

Key individuals from the departments providing the information will be responsible for the administration of it.

20. Day In A Pub Programme

Whilst part of the overall Succeeding with Customers & Quality Policy, its aim is partially to increase Corporate (non-Retail) employees' awareness of the Company's core business.

It is to be used as a means of fostering two-way communications between the centre and retail outlet employees.

DOCUMENT No: 3.4	Organisation Document	Bass Taverns Employee Communication Policy (p7)

21. Audio Tapes

These will be used for conveying "live" messages about the business to those employees who are frequently on the road.

The aim will be to produce at least two per annum.

22. Video

This will be used for Annual Results plus special one-offs for major change/issues. In addition, it will be used for communiques from senior management who are unable to present 'live' to their target audiences, and where abstract subject matter requires consistent presentation and/or benefits from visualisation.

23. Winners

"Winners" will be recognised for their success and "winning" will be encouraged wherever possible. Entering awards/competitions, by individuals, outlets or corporately is to be encouraged and help given by PR/Communications in producing high quality applications. PR will also co-ordinate entries for high profile industry awards such as the "Publican" and "Licensee" awards and will work with other functions, such as HR for the National Training Awards.

Recognition of Winners will be via the Core Brief (including Mystery Customer successes), Inn Touch, Certificates in Reception Areas — particularly the Cape Hill Reception Area where certificate display is a focal point of the design — local presentations and at the National Conference. Press releases will be distributed to local regional media wherever appropriate.

DOCUMENT No: 3.5   Description (p1)

Organisation ICL
Document Internal communications planning framework

Target Audiences and Key Characteristics	Objectives of Communication	Key Messages	Actions and Behaviours to Demonstrate your message	Methods to be Used and Timing	Feedback and Measurement	Cost
Specify the key characteristics of the people you are going to communicate with. Eg older employees anxious, cynical, aggressive, fear change	Use this column to work out what you are trying to achieve by communicating with these audiences. Eg To obtain involvement and buy in. To assist in the understanding of (x) business decision.	What are your key messages. This column should help you keep them succinct and simple Eg Company is changing focus towards a services business. We need to retrain and re-skill to be more competitive	Consider how you are going to make your message come alive, how is it to be demonstrated Eg Retraining workshops organised on customer focus and role model bahaviours. Sanctions applied to all people who do not demonstrate the correct behaviours	How are you going to communicate to these target audiences. Consider timings and locations as well as the context of the message Eg Company workshops/ roadshows. Face to face briefing	Build a feedback forum into every one of your communication channels. Qualify and quantify the feedback Eg Focus Groups, interactive feedback. Questions and answer session, recorded and passed up the organisation. Communication loop closed with downward feedback	Cost should not just be measured in pounds and pence but in time spent too. Eg 6 hours. 2 hours middle mgmt 1 hour senior mgmt

DOCUMENT No: 3.5

Organisation Document — ICL
Internal communications planning framework (p2)

Target Audiences and Key Characteristics	Objectives of Communication	Key Messages	Actions and Behaviours to Demonstrate your message	Methods to be Used and Timing	Feedback and Measurement	Cost
Create as many columns as you have target audiences	To keep them involved in the decision making process	The services business needs new skills and role model behaviour	Role models identified and promoted	Face to face briefing	Question and answer session, see above	See above
Middle Management aware, proactive, supportive, etc	To facilitate onward communication of the key message	All employees are to be involved	Mandate attendance at all training	Training workshops	Feedback sheets Trainer to constantly check for understanding and feedback issues arising	£500 per day for trainer £10,000 to develop course 380 hours of middle mgmt time
				Audio tape Business TV	Quarterly Communication audit	£10,000 per quarter, 21 hours time

DOCUMENTS

107

DOCUMENT No: 3.6

Organisation Nynex

Document Description Internal Communication Activity Checklist plus examples of documents used during the flotation process (p1)

NYNEX CableComms flotation

Internal Communication Activity Checklist

28 Feb	Internal News Release 6/95
	Message on Hotline
	Letter to every staff member's home
	Senior manager's brief - letter, key points, Q&A
	Customer Service staff brief
15 May	Prospectus, Q&A and Application form letter to staff members' home
	Internal News Release 22/95
16 May	Team Brief 17 initiated
22 May	CableComments staff magazine published
16 June	Employee Share Option Plan certificate mailing
19 June	Halifax Sharesave scheme brochure mailing
20 June	Team Brief 18 initiated
13 July	CableComments staff magazine published
26 July	Sharesave scheme certificates mailing

Other activity not enclosed includes the various certificate mailings (e g ESOP allocations)

DOCUMENT No: 3.6	Organisation Document	Nynex Internal Communication Flotation documents (p2)

To: *managers2
From:
Subject: URGENT NEWS
Date: 2/27/95   Time: 11:10a

To all level 2 Managers and above

An important message from EC is being couriered to your work location overnight tonight, Monday 27 February. It will be delivered by 8.30am latest, addressed personally to individual managers, to your office reception for collection by you or your nominated representative. Please note that the content is embargoed until 8am, Tuesday 28 February and should remain confidential until that time.

If you are not at your normal place of work tomorrow morning, will you please make arrangements to have the package forwarded to you by a colleague. The contents should not be transmitted by fax until after 8am Tuesday and then not without someone being in a position to receive it.

If, for any reason, a manager who is entitled to one does not receive a pack, their own manager is authorised to provide them with a copy of their own.

(name)
118 283

DOCUMENT No: 3.6
Organisation Nynex

Document   Internal Communication Flotation
documents (p3)

INTERNAL NEWS RELEASE

A service from NYNEX Internal Communication   118 027

Ref:6/95/CC   *28 February 1995*

NYNEX CABLECOMMS ANNOUNCES INTENTION TO FLOAT

At 8 am today, Tuesday, 28 February, NYNEX CableComms Group ("CableComms") announced its intention to seek a listing on both the London Stock Exchange and on the National Association of Securities Dealers Automated Quotation National Market System (Nasdaq) in New York as part of an international public offer of shares in CableComms.

President Gene Connell, who has written to all staff, said:

"I am informing you of this exciting development in CableComms' future at the first opportunity that rules and regulations permit. Up to this point we have been advised that we should not respond to media speculation about the flotation until a decision to proceed was taken. The decision to proceed has now been made.

"The flotation will have no effect on the terms of your employment. It will provide CableComms and the other companies in the group with funds to expand our operations so that we can take advantage of the opportunities in our chosen areas of business."

He also indicated that employees will be given the opportunity to participate in the flotation through a preferential share application scheme.

Detailed timings of the flotation programme remain subject to confirmation, so it is not possible to give you more detail at this stage. Departmental managers will endeavour to answer any early questions. Customer Services managers have a brief for their staff to give guidance in dealing with customer enquiries.

For further information, contact either   or   at Corporate Communications, Wimbledon.

You are strongly advised to read the statements set out below.

This advertisement, which has been prepared and issued by NYNEX CableComms Limited, has been approved by S.G.Warburg & Co. Ltd. and Salomon Brothers International Limited, members of The Securities and Futures Authority, for the purposes of section 57 of the Financial Services Act 1986. No offer or invitation to acquire securities of NYNEX CableComms Group PLC or NYNEX CableComms Group Inc. is being made now. Any such offer or invitation will be made in listing particulars to be published in due course and any such acquisition should be made solely on the basis of information contained in such listing particulars. S.G.Warburg & Co. Ltd. and Salomon Brothers International Limited are advising NYNEX CableComms Limited in relation to the offer and no one else and will not be responsible to anyone other than NYNEX CableComms Limited for providing the protections afforded to customers of S.G.Warburg & Co. Ltd. or Salomon Brothers International Limited nor for providing advice in relation to the offer. The value of securities and shares can fluctuate. For advice consult a professional adviser.

NOTICE: Not for use/disclosure outside NYNEX except by written agreement.

110

DOCUMENT No: 3.6 Organisation Nynex
Document Internal Communication Flotation
documents (p4)

NYNEX CableComms Limited
The Tolworth Tower
Ewell Road
Surbiton
Surrey KT6 7ED

Telephone 0181-873 2000
Facsimile 0181-390 9993

NYNEX

28 February 1995

Dear Colleague,

Today, we are announcing that NYNEX CableComms Group ("CableComms") is
to seek a listing on both the London Stock Exchange and on the National
Association of Securities Dealers Automated Quotation National Market
System (Nasdaq) in New York as part of an international public offer of
shares in CableComms.

I am informing you of this exciting development in Cable Comms' future at
the first opportunity that rules and regulations permit. We have made every
effort to ensure that you receive the news first from CableComms for it is
likely that stories will now start to appear in national and local newspapers.
Up to this point, we have been advised that we should not respond to media
speculation about the flotation until a decision to proceed was taken. The
decision to proceed has now been made.

The flotation will have no effect on the terms of your employment. It will
provide CableComms and the other companies in the group with funds to
expand our operations so that we can take advantage of the opportunities in
our chosen areas of business.

All CableComms employees will be given the opportunity to participate in the
flotation by purchasing shares in CableComms through a preferential share
application scheme. You will be given full details as soon as they become
available.

The detailed timings of the flotation programme remain subject to
confirmation, so it is not possible to give you more details at this stage. Your
departmental managers will endeavour to answer any early questions.

cont'd..../

Registered in England No. 2664006

Registered Office: Wimbledon Bridge House
1 Hartfield Road • Wimbledon • SW19 3RU

NYNEX CableComms Limited is the agent
of associated companies including those
licensed under the Telecommunications
and Broadcasting Acts

DOCUMENT No: 3.6

Organisation Nynex

Document   Internal Communication Flotation
documents (p5)

The company is receiving financial advice in connection with the flotation from a team which includes the leading City firms of S.G.Warburg & Co. Ltd. and Salomon Brothers International Limited and some of you may already have been in touch with representatives of these firms. If you are approached by members of the press or customers for information about the flotation it is extremely important that you do not reply to any of their enquiries. They must be directed to either Simon Bond (118 - 015), Jean Sawyer (118 - 016), Allen Saunders (118 - 260) or Adrian Seward (118 - 283) at Wimbledon.

This is a milestone in the history of CableComms and I would like to extend my personal thanks to you all for your efforts which have enabled us to take this significant step forward.

Yours sincerely,

Eugene P. Connell

Eugene P. Connell
President and Chief Executive Officer

You are strongly advised to read the statements set out below.

This advertisement, which has been prepared and issued by NYNEX CableComms Limited, has been approved by S.G.Warburg & Co. Ltd. and Salomon Brothers International Limited, members of The Securities and Futures Authority, for the purposes of section 57 of the Financial Services Act 1986. No offer or invitation to acquire securities of NYNEX CableComms Group PLC or NYNEX CableComms Group Inc. is being made now. Any such offer or invitation will be made in listing particulars to be published in due course and any such acquisition should be made solely on the basis of information contained in such listing particulars. S.G.Warburg & Co. Ltd. and Salomon Brothers International Limited are advising NYNEX CableComms Limited in relation to the offer and no one else and will not be responsible to anyone other than NYNEX Cablecomms Limited for providing the protections afforded to customers of S.G.Warburg & Co. Ltd. or Salomon Brothers International Limited nor for providing advice in relation to the offer. The value of securities and shares can fluctuate. For advice consult a professional adviser.

DOCUMENT No: 3.6

Organisation Document	Nynex Internal Communication Flotation documents (p6)

NYNEX CableComms Limited
Wimbledon Bridge House
1 Hartfield Road
Wimbledon SW19 3RU

Telephone 081 540 8833
Facsimile 081 544 0811

28 February 1995

NYNEX

Dear Colleague,

The announcement that NYNEX CableComms Group ("CableComms") is to seek a listing on both the London Stock Exchange and on Nasdaq in New York is a milestone in our development. Your directors believe this is a positive initiative and hope that employees see it that way too.

We are keen to maintain good communication with all staff during this process, consequently we are asking you, and all other senior managers, to brief staff shortly after the announcement that CableComms is to seek a listing has been made. This announcement is to be at 8am on Tuesday, February 28, 1995.

Your directors acknowledge that detailed information is not yet available and that it is therefore difficult for you to be anything other than general in what you say. However, I feel it will be helpful for staff to know that the company regards their support in the run up to flotation and beyond as extremely valuable and we want everyone to continue to be motivated. It will also be helpful for them to have no doubt that when we are able to say more to them, we will do so.

To equip you for your briefing, please find attached some key points and a question and answer document which is intended for your personal use only. It must not be circulated either inside or outside the company. It has been prepared by our advisors and meets the regulatory requirements that we are duty bound to follow. If you receive any enquiries from the press or customers concerning the flotation, it is extremely important that they be referred to either Simon Bond (118 - 015), Jean Sawyer (118 - 016), Allen Saunders (118 - 260) or Adrian Seward (118 - 283) at Wimbledon.

We will be in touch again shortly, and in the coming weeks you will receive further information on this subject to enable you to brief your staff in more detail.

Yours sincerely,

Eugene P. Connell
President and Chief Executive Officer

113

Key points for senior managers' brief

- NYNEX Cablecomms Group ("CableComms") has today announced to the media its intention to seek a listing on the London Stock Exchange and Nasdaq in New York as part of an international public offer of shares in CableComms. The process is described as a flotation. CableComms believes this is positive news because it should provide funds to help expand operations and to develop our business further.

- Having made the decision to seek a listing, CableComms wanted to inform employees first. With this in mind, a letter from the President was posted to arrive at the homes of employees today, hopefully ahead of likely media interest. An Internal News Release will go out on the PC network on Tuesday morning.

- Now that a decision has been taken, CableComms is legally required to observe rules and regulations which limit the information we can give. It is also a fact that timings and full details have yet to be confirmed.

- Employees will be given an opportunity to participate in the flotation by purchasing shares in CableComms. Once there is more detailed information on this, you will receive it. In the meantime, there is nothing you need to do.

- Flotation will not affect your job with the company. This is all about funding future expansion and the senior management hopes you will share its view that the news is exciting, and will help CableComms and the other companies in the group to grow further.

DOCUMENT No: 3.6	Organisation Document	Nynex Internal Communication Flotation documents (p8)

Qs and As:

Q1   What is flotation and what does it mean to me?

A1   Flotation is the term used for the process by which a public limited company (PLC) is listed on a Stock Exchange following which institutions (such as pension funds and insurance companies) and individuals are able to buy and sell shares in the company. NYNEX CableComms Group ("CableComms") is seeking a listing on both the London Stock Exchange and Nasdaq in New York, following which it will be required to present detailed and accurate information on its business and financial performance in a prospectus to shareholders and potential shareholders and to publish financial results on a regular basis. CableComms' share price will be quoted on the London Stock Exchange and Nasdaq and you will be able to see this share price in the newspapers. The flotation will enable CableComms to raise funds for future expansion and will also raise its profile among the general public.

Q2   Is my job safe?

A2   This development will make absolutely no difference to your job security. As always, the critical factor is how well CableComms and you as an individual perform.

Q3   How are my terms and conditions affected?

A3   They are unaffected.

Q4   What happens to my pension?

A4   This is unaffected too.

Q5   Will I be required to work differently?

A5   Not as a direct result of the flotation. However, as you know, CableComms and the individuals in it have a policy of continuous improvement in all that we do.

Q5a   Are we likely to be taken over as a result?

A5a   No. NYNEX Corporation will continue to hold a majority interest in CableComms following the flotation.

Q6   Why is CableComms taking this step?

A6   Because we believe that as all the businesses of CableComms are in the UK, CableComms will benefit from being partially owned by British shareholders and employees, rather than being totally American owned. The capital raised through the issue of shares on flotation will also mean that we are in a better position to fund future expansion. We believe it is in CableComms' best interests to seek a listing so that we can take full advantage of the many opportunities on which we are focused.

Q7   Will we be changing our name?

A7   That is not a consideration at present.

Q8   What are our prospects?

A8   We will be detailing our prospects in the prospectus which is to be published in due course. Speaking generally, we feel we are well placed for the future development of our business if we continue to do all the things we are good at. There is no shortage of opportunities.

Q9   What are we supposed to say to customers?

A9   Apart from a general "We regard this as good news and a positive development", it is most important that you make no other specific comments. At this stage, you should only give information which you have been told is legally approved for circulation. Refer enquiries to the customer services managers Southern Region, Northern Region.

Q10   Is the management changing?

A10   There are no plans for significant management changes.

DOCUMENT No: 3.6	Organisation	Nynex
	Document	Internal Communication Flotation documents (p10)

Q11   How can I purchase shares in CableComms?

A11   A preferential share application scheme for employees will be available and further information will be given on this once timings are known and details are approved. Other schemes for employees may also be made available.

Q12   What will be the price at which shares are offered?

A12   It has not yet been decided. You will be informed as soon as this information is available.

Q13   What changes will I see as a result of flotation?

A13   Essentially, nothing will change internally. You will probably be aware of increased media coverage and customer interest in CableComms.

DOCUMENTS

DOCUMENT No: 3.6

Organisation Nynex

Document   Internal Communication Flotation
documents (p11)

INTERNAL NEWS RELEASE

A service from NYNEX Internal Communication   155 248

15 May 1995

Ref:22/95/CC

This announcement is not for distribution in the United States, Canada or Japan.

NYNEX CableComms Group ("CableComms")
Global Combined Offering to raise between £400 million and £460 million

NYNEX CableComms announces the launch today of its flotation by means of an international equity offering.

- CableComms is raising between £400 million and £460 million (before expenses) through an issue of 305 million equity Units. It is expected that the Units will be priced at between 131p and 151p each.

- The market capitalisation of CableComms following the Combined Offering is expected to be between approximately £1.2 billion and £1.4 billion.

- The Combined Offering comprises a U.K. and International Offering of 183 million Units (60 per cent. of the Units being offered) and a U.S. Offering of 122 million Units (40 per cent. of the Units being offered). The Units will be listed on the London Stock Exchange and traded in ADS form on Nasdaq in New York.

- CableComms is the second largest multiple systems operator in the U.K. It has managerial and operational control over all its franchises.

- CableComms is licensed to provide cable television and telecommunications services in 16 franchise areas covering approximately 2.7 million homes, equivalent to approximately 17 per cent. of total franchised homes in the U.K.

- Approximately 1.7 million of CableComms' franchise homes are located within ten franchises in and around Manchester and are managed and operated as a single system. Of the other six franchises, one is in Derby, two are in the London area, and three are along the south coast of England.

- NYNEX Corporation will not sell any Units in the Combined Offering and will hold approximately 67 per cent. of CableComms following the Combined Offering.

- Joint global co-ordinators of the Combined Offering are S.G. Warburg and Salomon Brothers.

Eugene Connell, President and Chief Executive Officer of CableComms, commented:

"I am delighted to announce another significant step in the development of our business. We are convinced that the future for CableComms is an exciting one and are pleased to offer new investors and our employees the opportunity to share together with NYNEX in our group's prospects. We look forward to the challenge of building our business further with the support, and for the benefit, of all our future shareholders."

A special mailing to the home addresses of all CableComms employees is being sent out today.

For more information contact   **in Tolworth on**

This announcement, which has been prepared and issued by NYNEX CableComms Group PLC and NYNEX CableComms Group Inc., has been approved by S.G. Warburg Securities Ltd. and Salomon Brothers International Limited, members of The Securities and Futures Authority, for the purposes of section 57 of the Financial Services Act 1986. Stabilisation/SIB.

NOTICE: Not for use/disclosure outside NYNEX except by written agreement.

DOCUMENT No: 3.6 | Organisation Document | Nynex Internal Communication Flotation documents (p12)

CABLECOMMENTS ● JUNE-JULY 1995   VOLUME 4 NUMBER 3

CableComments
NYNEX

Flotation success is 'team effort'

An open letter from the President

Eugene P Connell

YOU were no doubt as pleased as I was on June 9 to learn that we had achieved the successful flotation of NYNEX CableComms on the London and New York Stock Exchanges.

For three hectic weeks I was privileged to lead a group of my colleagues around the UK, Europe and the USA to present our case to the major investors and analysts who were critical to the success of the flotation. Convincing such people to buy into a business as young as ours in a very new industry is by no means a foregone conclusion and I am conscious that everyone back home in CableComms made a considerable effort to ensure that we achieved our goal.

Investors can never be wholly convinced by the presentations that are the most visible part of the flotation process – they want to know that there is confidence, ability and a robust track record throughout the company and that is how we made the flotation a team success.

I cannot thank you all personally for playing your part in helping us reach our goal and it is not appropriate for me to single out any individuals but I am really proud to put on record my gratitude to each one of you for your part in bringing the company to a place where we could achieve this major goal.

We floated at the right price, that price stayed stable as trading in difficult market conditions started and we are now a company valued at £1.3bn.

I am confident that we will enjoy the fruits of what we have done together as we move our new company forward into the future.

NYNEX stamps its name on Arena deal

NYNEX has won the race to put its name on Europe's largest indoor sports and entertainment complex.

The £56 million, 19,500-seat complex opens on July 15 under the name NYNEX Arena Manchester as part of a deal which will give CableComms extensive marketing, promotional and sales opportunities – plus bring in substantial telecomms revenue into the next century.

The five-year 'naming rights' contract with Ogden Entertainment Services – part of the Ogden Corporation, world leaders in venue management – was won in the face of competition from a number of well-known national and international companies.

The CableComms bid, put together

Turn to Page 3

Celebrating the Arena deal are, from left, Adrian Weatherby, General Manager Business Markets, Lee Esckilsen, Arena Executive Director, and John Knight, Head of PR - North, with supporting cheerleaders and basketball players

TIMETABLE

Day one

AM   Senior Management Briefing (Management Committee and Divisional Chief Executives).

PM   Human Resources advised of details of redundancy

- Agreement with Heads of Function as to who will brief.

- Support available for day two PM meetings.

Day two

AM   Support for PM meetings.

PM   Heads of Function or deputies to brief:

- Managers who are redundant themselves and have to brief others on redundancy

- Managers who are not themselves redundant, but who have to brief others on redundancy.

Day three

- Any outstanding issues to be discussed with Group Human Resources (eg clarification of the brief).

- Outstanding questions from the sessions on day one.

- Timetable arranged between briefing managers and Human Resources on the day of announcement.

DOCUMENT No: 3.7	Organisation Document	Unattributed Communication redundancy plan (p2)

Day four - Announcement Day

0900   Managers make arrangements for meeting schedule

0930   Managers brief individually persons affected by redundancy

- *as soon as this process is completed Managers will brief those remaining on how the department is affected*

- Managers will then E-mail the Human Resources department on completion of this segment of the activity.

1600   Cascade briefing to all employees on the restructured organisation within the company.

1630   Announcement released to other Group companies.

Day five

- Individual discussions between manager and redundant staff on working arrangements between now and date of the redundancies taking effect.

- Individuals who are required to work beyond this date should be advised as soon as possible.

- Pensions and HR staff available for consultation on appropriate matters by appointment.

MANAGERS BRIEFING GUIDE FOR ANNOUNCEMENT INTERVIEW

1 Organisational situation (notes to help open the interview)

1.1 Interim results statement explained the difficulties we were experiencing.

1.2 In recent weeks a major review of activity has been undertaken which has resulted in a clear understanding of our future role and how we can best cost effectively add value.

1.3 This has resulted in a number of changes.

2 Chairman's statement

2.1 Read out statement.

3 Redundancy

3.1 I have to give you notice of our intention to terminate your employment for reasons of redundancy on (date).

3.2 The reason that you have been chosen is that your position.......

3.3 The terms of payment that will be made to you are as outlined.

3.4 We would like you to work through until (date), when your employment would cease and you separation payment would be available.

3.5 If you wish to leave before then, we would need to have further discussion to mutually agree an alternative date.

3.6 We will provide you with outplacement support and details will be made available to you shortly if you wish to take advantage of this. Additionally we will make efforts to review the possibility of professional employment within other parts of the company.

DOCUMENTS

4   What happens next?

4.1   We will meet again during the next few days, but certainly within the next 3 days to finalise your arrangements including your car and any other property matters.

4.2   Pensions and HR will be available to discuss appropriate details   and support but please make an appointment.

At this stage a check should be made that the message of redundancy has been understood.

5   Briefing

5.1   We are advising you of your own situation in advance of a general announcement, when.........in your department will also be made redundant.

5.2   It is appropriate that you have the necessary discussions with....... There would be understanding if you felt unable to do this, but I would like your decision by tomorrow if you feel unable to do this.

5.3   The briefing to all affected employees will be held individually with departmental meetings being held late the same day where the revised structure will be discussed. You are obviously invited to attend this meeting.

5.4   A departmental meeting will be held at 1600 today to provide details of the revised Head Office structure. You are obviously invited to attend this meeting.

5.5   Finally, we will meet again shortly, so we can organise diaries to do that now please.

DOCUMENTS

MANAGERS BRIEFING GUIDE

1 Organisation Situation (Notes to help open the interview)

1.1 Interim results statement explained the difficulties we were experiencing.

1.2 In recent weeks a major review of activity has been undertaken. This has resulted in a clear understanding of our future role on how we cost effectively add value.

1.3 This has resulted in a number of changes.

2 Chairman's statement

2.1 Read out statement.

3 How this affects us

3.1 As a consequence I have had to advise (name of affected) of our intention to terminate their employment due to the redundancy of their position from (date).

3.2 While it is not appropriate to discuss details, I can assure you that the individuals have been treated well and the payments which will be made are in excess of the statutory minimum we are required to pay through law.

3.3 This discussion is part of a cascade communication throughout the company today, and must remain confidential until after the 1600 meeting as other departments may not have seen everybody until this time.

3.4 There will be a further meeting of the department at 1600.

DOCUMENT No: 3.7

Organisation Document

Unattributed
Communication redundancy plan
(p6)

DEPARTMENTAL BRIEF

1 Introduction

1.1 You have all now been seen to explain your own circumstances, as have all of our colleagues in other departments.

1.2 The following announcement is being made to the rest of the company at 1630 today. **(Read out organisational announcement.)**

1.3 As a result of the decisions advised today, all departments are now organised as follows......
and unfortunately these employees will be leaving over the next few weeks **(overheads to be prepared)**.

ORGANISATION ANNOUNCEMENT FOR OPERATING COMPANIES

The difficult trading conditions which we announced at our interim results have shown no signs of improvement. This has necessitated in severe headcount reductions across most of the Group during the last quarter.

As a consequence we have undergone a thorough review of the number of people we employ.

It is therefore with regret that I have to announce that...... amount of our people have been declared redundant today.

I remain convinced that the long term prospects for the company remain excellent and by working together we will achieve the necessary improvements in order to satisfy our customers and take advantage of the growth opportunities when they return.

DOCUMENT No: 3.8

Organisation Parcelforce
Document Joint internal/external communication plan

Description Extracts from communication plan showing joint planning of internal/external activities and messages (p1)

MESSAGES

	STRATEGIC MESSAGES	KEY INTERNAL MESSAGES	KEY EXTERNAL MESSAGES
A.	Financial Performance.	Parcelforce is now operating profitably - a major achievement, which all our staff should be proud of. We now need to build further on our break-even position to ensure our future in a highly competitive market.	Parcelforce has moved rapidly from heavy losses to financial viability in the face of very difficult market conditions. Unlike many of its competitors Parcelforce's financial results do not reflect any cross-subsidy from sister businesses or its parent company.
B.	Job Security/Good Employer.	Working conditions in Parcelforce are among the most favourable in the distribution industry. The future of Parcelforce is firmly in the hands of its employees: we stand or fall by our performance in the market place.	Parcelforce has achieved radical change without any compulsory redundancy.
C.	Flexibility.	Working practices in Parcelforce must be geared to the needs of the customer, who pays our wages. Employees have the ability to enhance their take-home pay by exceeding target levels of performance. Parcelforce will take full account of the circumstances of its staff in planning work schedules to meet customer needs.	Parcelforce has pioneered changes in working practices that enable it to be fully responsive to the needs of the customer.

DOCUMENT No: 3.8

Organisation
Document

Parcelforce
Joint internal/external communication
plan (p2)

STRATEGIC MESSAGES

KEY INTERNAL MESSAGES

KEY EXTERNAL MESSAGES

D. Quality.

In a network, operation achievement of agreed performance standards is vital at every stage of the pipeline.
Quality depends on all aspects of performance, and particularly on the ability to deliver information as well as parcels.

Parcelforce service performance compares well with that of competitors on a service-by-service basis.

Parcelforce is committed to providing market-leading quality in the widest sense of the word.

E. Technology.

Parcelforce has embarked on a programme of investment in tracking systems that will cover its entire service range, and put it at the forefront of the industry.

As for internal messages.

F. Customer Service.

Whether on the phone or face-to-face, the way we treat customers can make all the difference to whether we retain their business.
When we deliver parcels for our customers to their customers we are in effect representing them.
It's when something goes wrong that customers expect to get easy access to somebody who will own the problem, not fob them off.

Parcelforce prides itself on its standards of customer service and ease of access to its network. It is involved in major programmes to further improve its ability to meet customer needs.

(A)   CORE BUSINESS LEVEL PROGRAMME

SUBJECT	RATIONALE	INTERNAL ACTIVITY	EXTERNAL ACTIVITY	TIMING
Customer Service Perceptions.	To significantly boost customers' perception of the service performance PF provides.	Video extracts for BU briefings. Rapid Response team's recommendations. Action on long term standards. Posters, leaflets etc.	Above-the-line Advertising campaign.	May-September.
Flexible Working Practices.	To convey rationale and details of proposals to management and front-line staff.	Business Briefing. Courier scene setter. Insight feature. GM/MD Tape. Newsline.	One-to-one press briefings with selected journalists.	April - July (announcement)
Opinion Survey (follow-through) .	To publish outline results and convey commitment to follow-through.	Courier and Insight coverage, backed by detailed results for individual units and single sheet results summary.		May - June.
Royal Mail Staff briefings.	(i) To convey Parcelforce quality requirements to RM front-line staff. (ii) To set the partnership deal in the correct context.	Briefing to Royal Mail Business Units. Possible article in RM or Corporate sections of Courier.		April - June
Annual Results.	To position Parcelforce as making progress, and with a clear vision of the extent of change required.	Parcelforce Annual Review to senior managers. Courier special edition. Team briefings.	Selected media briefings linked to FWP. Parcelforce Annual Review for Customers and Trade Press.	June

DOCUMENT No: 3.8	Organisation Document	Parcelforce Joint internal/external communication plan (p4)

(G) OTHER

SUBJECT	RATIONALE	INTERNAL ACTIVITY	EXTERNAL ACTIVITY	TIMING
European Quality Award.	To enhance internal and external perceptions of Parcelforce's quality aspirations.	Briefing features on Parcelforce's entry and what it entails.	Media briefing, linked to other activities.	May .
Crisis Management.	Damage limitation.	Help to develop a new crisis recovery plan that ensures communications are adequately catered for.		May.
Environment.	To boost image of Parcelforce as a responsible company.	Courier and Insight will stress Parcelforce's continuing record as a responsible and enlightened corporate citizen.	News Releases/Features.	May onwards.
Post Office People in the Community.	To recognise the activities of Parcelforce's employees in their local communities.	Coverage in Courier of the "winners" plus letters of congratulations from managers. Management Brief.	Press Releases/Photocalls.	May - November.
Responsiveness.	Parcelforce's commitment to customer needs is manifested in new customised solutions division. Flexibility is a key factor in many, if not most major contract gains.	Courier and Insight.	Press Releases/Features. Joint customer activity.	Ad hoc.
People, profiles, appointments etc.'	To demonstrate business orientation, especially on quality and technology, and market focus.	Courier.	Press Releases. Speaking Opportunities. Photocall.	Ongoing.
Gold Depot and Sort Centre Awards.	To convey Parcelforce's commitment to quality.		Press Release/Photocalls and Features.	Ongoing.

DOCUMENT No: 3.9
Organisation   Lloyds Bank
Document   Communication standards

Description   Examples of communication
             standards (p1)

The Communication Standards

Our Internal Communication will be
measured against the following standards:

Honesty and Openness

- Top Management will undertake to
  explain:
  – the rationale
  – the facts and
  – the pros and cons
  of the decisions they take which affect
  us and the way we work together.

- We shall all be candid and open with
  each other. Admitting our mistakes
  and learning from them is a key part
  of this.

- It is everyone's responsibility to
  contribute towards a more open and
  honest working environment.

- Listening is an important skill for us all
  to learn and apply.

Feedback

- We shall all be able to give constructive
  feedback to and receive it from any
  of our colleagues, including our
  manager or senior management without
  fear of reprisals. Managers have a
  responsibility to encourage feedback.

- Everyone will receive a
  full and truthful response
  to their comments and questions.

- Open discussions between staff and
  management, at all levels, will take
  place on a regular basis.

  – Each General Manager and Regional
  Executive Director will chair meetings
  with staff and managers at least twice
  a year.

  – Area Directors and other Senior
  Executives will similarly meet with
  staff on a regular basis.

All issues will be communicated in line with these Standards, unless personal privacy, share price or commercial interests need to

Everyone's views will be sought regularly on how well the Standards are being met. This will take place through formal discussion

DOCUMENT No: 3.9

Organisation   Lloyds Bank
Document   Communication standards (p2)

Consistency, Clarity and Co-ordination

- We shall use plain English and avoid jargon.

- Central communication initiatives will be co-ordinated and the information they contain will be consistent.

- Written and spoken communication will be tailored to the requirements of the audience.

- Training will be made available for team leaders to enhance their communication skills. This will help them to write concisely, present ideas clearly and run meetings effectively.

Speed and Relevance

- We shall be informed of internal issues from Top Management at least as quickly as from external parties.

- Lloyds Bank will comment within two working days when news of relevance to its staff breaks outside the Bank first.

- We will all be advised of information that is relevant to us and our work.

- Information will be received first by those who need it most.

- Managers will communicate messages of local relevance and concern to their own teams, without delay.

be protected. There will be no comment on media speculation.

groups involving staff and managers and through staff attitude research. The results will be made available to all staff.

DOCUMENT No: 3.10   Description Examples of communication standards

Organisation   Cable and Wireless
Document   Communication standards

**CABLE & WIRELESS
BUSINESS NETWORKS**

Our Ten Communication Commitments

We commit to strive to ensure that the following principles of good internal communication are met:

1.   Reflecting the basis for our commercial success, the development of productive internal relationships is the key aim of internal communication.

2.   The primary customers for internal communication will be all C & W employees who serve the customers. Communication processes will be continually updated to meet their changing needs.

3.   Communication will be open, honest and realistic. Only information which the BNE decides, in exceptional circumstances, is too commercially sensitive will *not* be rapidly available to all BN members. There will be no restrictions on information sharing based on hierarchy. The management line will be primarily for discussion of information, rather than dissemination. *Personal personnel matters excluded.*

4.   Central BN will ensure that all members of BN can identify and reach each other readily (no more than two calls). (They will provide an up-to-date directory of BN personnel, their place in the structure/broad function and their names, telephone, E-mail, fax and hard addresses, so that anyone in the BN world can determine who the person is they need to speak to and reach them with no more than two calls).

5.   Technology investment will always be a top priority to ensure the rapid, free flow of accessible information internationally via efficient and structured E-mail systems, as well as video and audio conferencing.

6.   All staff have the right and the responsibility to be updated regularly at least quarterly on the direction, targets and performance of the business and to both receive good and challenging ("bad") news.

7.   All staff have the right to participate in regular (at least monthly) two-way discussions with their operational team and leader. Staff can elect which team discussion they are part of. The content and process of these meetings will be agreed between the team and its leader and reviewed quarterly. Staff also have the right to have a face-to-face group briefing and discussion opportunities with a member of the BNE at least three times a year.

8.   All staff have a responsibility to escalate potential and actual problems as rapidly as possible and to feed back to their team or senior managers positive and negative news/observations/ideas. Staff have the right to have these constructively received, not to be shot as the messenger and to receive a response on resulting action.

9.   Managers at all levels will aim to communicate in person as frequently as possible. Whilst channels for operational and non-emotive detail will be E-mail/fax or paper based, two-way telephone, video and face-to-face communication with staff will represent 50% of management time.

10.   Performance against these principles will be appraised on an individual and overall level annually, to identify opportunities for continuous improvement. This may include amendments to the principles.

DOCUMENT No: 3.11

Organisation   Nynex

Document Description   Communication standards
Examples of communication standards

the standards

introduction

One certainty that faces any organisation today is that change is constant. It is doubly so for a company like ours in such a highly competitive market. NYNEX needs to keep flexible to meet the changing needs of our market and the most effective way to achieve this is to create a customer oriented culture throughout our organisation and maintain an awareness among all of us of the value of high quality, relevant and timely communication. Effective communication will help us energise the whole organisation.

It will clarify our responsibilities.

It will identify appropriate training needs.

It will recognise and reward improvement.

And good communication will create customer satisfaction and loyalty.

These standards are the commitment of the management team to improving our internal communication. They have been drawn up through consultation across the workforce because we recognise that two-way communication is absolutely vital. The Standards will work when we all respect each other's needs and build a business which we understand, believe in and are committed to making a world class company.

I commend these Standards to you.

Eugene P Connell

Eugene P Connell

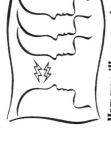

Why we will communicate

To help you do your job in a better, more informed way.

We want everyone to be aware of and involved with the progress of the Company.

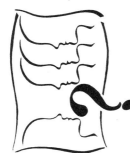
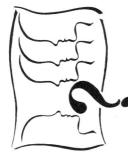

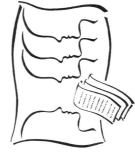

What we will communicate

Information that is relevant to your job.

Information about the Company that is of wider interest in the Company.

Regular updates on the key decisions, progress and plans of the Company,

How we will communicate

Communication will be two-way. Your views and opinions are valued. Management will give careful consideration of your ideas and will respond to you. Speaking up will not be held against you.

We will be accurate and honest in what we communicate.

The continuing need to maintain confidentiality in certain areas of our business will not be used as an excuse not to communicate.

We will make every piece of communication as concise as possible, consistent with it being clear and complete. You will be told where every piece of information has come from and where to obtain more information.

Everyone will be given the support they need to make the communication process successful.

Where we will communicate

Wherever possible, you will hear information that affects you and your job directly from your immediate manager.

Your manager will hold Team Meetings at least once a month. The manager's recognised deputy will run the meeting if the manager is not available. Team members who are unable to attend the meeting will be given the opportunity to speak with their manager separately.

We will continue to communicate through other means, such as CableComments and Internal News Releases, when these are more appropriate.

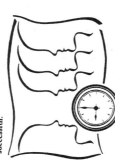

NYNEX®

When we will communicate

We will endeavour to make sure that you receive information as soon as we are able to tell you.

DOCUMENTS

DOCUMENT No: 3.12	Description	Examples of communication standards

Organisation Automobile Association
Document Speak up on issues

SPEAK UP ON ISSUES

COMMUNICATION

Effective internal communication is more than passing on information. It is about ensuring understanding, commitment and involvement. This is most likely to be the case when communication is two-way, open and face-to-face, which is why we have established the communication standards that are set out in full below.

We are all entitled to:

Updated information on our business and the AA

Make sure that you communicate what people want and need to know. Don't just dump information on them - customise the message and its meaning for each audience.

Regular meetings with our immediate manager

These need to be held on an individual or team basis so that information, views and ideas can be exchanged. AA Briefing is a monthly requirement for all managers. It provides a regular mechanism for you to communicate face-to-face with people, individually or as a team. Plan and prepare for it.

Raise concerns with our manager

Deal with issues raised with you promptly and fairly, and keep people informed of progress. Be accessible. Your "door" does not always need to be open but make it easy for people to see you with a minimum of formality. Then avoid distractions and interruptions and give them undivided attention.

Be consulted and involved

This relates to the improvement of our own and the AA's performance. Invariably, high levels of involvement lead to better solutions and results.

Face-to-face discussion about our performance

Monitor performance and review progress on a regular basis. If you provide feedback face-to-face there should be "no surprises" at the more formal performance reviews. After each of these, there is a requirement for a written summary that is honest, fair and accurate.

Be given the necessary responsibility and authority to do our job

A general rule is to give people as much responsibility as they can handle, and an equal measure of authority to carry it out effectively.

In return, we must:

Take an active and positive part in two-way communication

Try to make *all* communication two-way. Stimulate discussion and dialogue, and encourage people to raise ideas, suggestions and issues of concern to them.

Updated information on our business and the AA

Speak up on issues. Reinforce and demonstrate that feedback and responsible free speech is valued in the AA and carries no penalties. Encourage people to put forward solutions, not just problems.

Safeguard confidential information

Be as open as possible in keeping people informed on matters that are important to them. Don't breach confidentiality or hurt people unnecessarily but be objective and honest or your credibility will suffer

Make known our suggestions and ideas

When people have given you the benefit of their ideas and views, take the necessary follow-up action and keep them informed, whatever the outcome. If you tacitly ignore constructive feedback it will cease, and cynicism will replace it.

Express our feelings positively and honestly

"Telling it like it is" is always the best policy – provided it is done with thought and care.

Speak out against rumour, and speak up for the AA

Don't knock the organisation or fuel rumour and gossip. People should find out things from you as their manager, not hear them through the grapevine. They may need to keep what you tell them confidential for a period but your trust will inevitably be respected.

Regularly discuss our performance and development with our manager

Don't just wait for formal reviews - provide feedback on performance and development whenever it is appropriate. Listen as well as talk to understand where the other person is coming from.

Finally, two important reminders on being an effective communicator:

- Being visible is important and involves you making the effort to visit people from time to time. It demonstrates that what they are doing matters, and that you are interested and involved. "Walking the job" is important, but you need to have a purpose and do it regularly.

- Don't forget lateral communication. If you don't liaise and communicate with your peer group network in other parts of the business and group, problems will arise. Keeping close to internal suppliers and customers is also important.

DOCUMENT No: 3.13	Document Description	Understanding Process An example of best practice in two way communication (p1)
Organisation National and Provincial Building Society		

THE UNDERSTANDING PROCESS

PURPOSE OF THIS DOCUMENT

The purpose of this document is to enable players to fully understand the Understanding Process and their role within it.

PURPOSE OF THE UNDERSTANDING PROCESS

It is through the Understanding Process that we:

♦ Acquire understanding of our Direction
♦ Understand the contribution required of us to achieve our Direction
♦ Participate in the continuous improvement of our own and other teams and of the organisation as a whole
♦ Learn about the effectiveness of our team play

HOW WE CREATE UNDERSTANDING

Whilst communication is a vital ingredient of creating understanding, we believe that it is only part of the story. A common understanding, shared by all, is only achieved when everyone engages in a two-way dialogue of question, debate and challenge centred around shared information, ideas, issues, and achievements.

It is for this reason that we place such emphasis upon bringing players together in team events as part of the process for creating understanding.

TEAM EVENTS

Team events provide a time and a place where, through dialogue, understanding can be shared, team effectiveness reviewed, ideas for improvement put forward and issues and concerns about blockages to effectiveness raised.

To enable understanding to be shared quickly, and to facilitate business planning, the events take place regularly (ever two weeks) on a pre-determined schedule.

The events also take place in a particular sequence with understanding originating from DMP events, and moving through IMP events into IP events. The facilitator of each event will always have attended an event earlier in the sequence so that the continuity and integrity of the process is maintained.

DOCUMENT No: 3.13 Document Understanding process (p2)

Organisation National and Provincial Building Society

DIRECTION MANAGEMENT PROCESS EVENTS

At the conclusion of each consideration, DMP agree the understanding that needs to be shared throughout the organisation. These outputs are captured in the form of an Aide Memoire which becomes the input to all subsequent understanding events.

The Aide Memoire is designed to "jog the memory" of players who will be facilitating understanding events. It enables them to articulate the outputs of DMP. It is not intended to be a written briefing statement but rather an input to team events to facilitate dialogue about the implementation of Direction.

"STAGE 1" AND "STAGE 2" EVENTS

In the IMP, or "Stage 1" understanding events Process Leaders facilitate their team's understanding of Direction. Stage 2 (IP) events are facilitated by IP or Team Leaders.

All team understanding events follow the same basic format that is described below.

THE FORMAT OF UNDERSTANDING EVENTS

Firstly teams capture on flipchart their responses to the three "understanding questions":

> *What have we not done well (that we can improve)?*
>
> *What have we done well (that we can learn from)?*
>
> *Any issues, concerns or ideas.*

These questions can be applied to any aspect of the organisation such as a team, an individual player, feedback received from customers, a particular process or even the organisation as a whole. However, whilst the focus of the responses to the first two questions tends to be within the team, the final question encourages responses in relation both to the immediate team *and* the wider "team of teams".

All inputs are valid and to create a common understanding they are recorded on flip-chart using agreed and complete sentences which can be fully understood by the team *and any other team which may read them*.

At this point there is no challenge to the issues other than for clarity and understanding (challenge of the validity of the issues will come in point 3 below).

Secondly the facilitator leads a consideration of the implementation of Direction using the Aide Memoire to support their articulation. Team players contribute where they can add value and ask questions where they are unclear. Whilst those players at the event who will be taking the understanding forward to their own teams have a particular responsibility to challenge and question their understanding (so that they can convey it to others), everyone present at the event must ensure that they understand. It is as much the individual's responsibility to ensure understanding as it is the facilitator's.

Thirdly, the team works back through the responses to the three understanding questions in the light of the Aide Memoire consideration, agreeing the appropriate learning, action or response to each of the items raised *and improving the clarity of the wording if required*. Unresolved issues should be input to a specific and appropriate team or player (see the section on "Resolving Issues" below).

Where a response to a previously raised issue has been received from an another team, this should be shared with the team.

THE ROLE OF THE EVENT FACILITATOR

All players have a responsibility to ensure that the team develops its understanding and improves its effectiveness. However, the event facilitator has specific responsibilities for:

◆ **Ensuring that events are organised and publicised and that players attend.**

◆ **Leading the team's consideration of the Aide Memoire and of the players' issues.**

◆ **Ensuring that quality outputs are captured and distributed (including a copy to the Opportunities To Improve Team - See section on "Tools to Aid Issues Management" below).**

◆ **Ensuring that issues are fully considered and appropriate learning, actions and responses agreed.**

◆ **Ensuring that unresolved issues are actioned and followed through by agreed members of the team.**

◆ **Feeding back to the team the status of previously raised issues, including any responses received.**

◆ **Facilitating the team in such a way as to ensure full participation and contribution from all the players.**

◆ **Leading a consideration on the effectiveness of the team.**

DOCUMENT No: 3.13 Document   Understanding process (p4)

Organisation   National and Provincial Building Society

MANAGING AND RESOLVING ISSUES

The team raising an issue has the responsibility to try - as far as it is able - to resolve the issue for itself. Team effectiveness, learning and improvement do not come from "passing the buck"!

The team, therefore, challenges itself over every issue raised at the event by asking the question "Can we learn from and resolve this issue ourselves?" If the answer proves to be "No" the team considers the clarity of the wording of the issue (as it will now need to be understood by another team), as well as which other team or player is most appropriate to respond. However, it is important to note that even when the team cannot resolve an issue themselves they may still be able to learn from it (eg from the way they engaged a customer on the issue) and therefore the potential learning should always form a part of their consideration of the issue.

A specified member of the team then passes the unresolved issue to the agreed team or player - direct - by means of memo, E-mail or phone. It is the responsibility of that same player to follow-through the issue until a response is received, whereupon they share it with their team.

Teams keep a log of the issues (and their status) that they have passed to other teams, to facilitate follow-through.

Where a response to an issue is required urgently, before the next event, the appropriate team should be contacted direct. The issue should nevertheless be raised at the next event and the response shared with the team.

Those who receive issues from another team:

◆ **Consider the issue, preferably with their team**

◆ **Agree the action / improvement required**

◆ **Prepare a response describing the outcome of the consideration**

◆ **Take responsibility for feeding the response back to the originating team, as soon as possible, the action that has been taken**

TOOLS TO AID ISSUES MANAGEMENT

It is the facilitator's responsibility to ensure that a copy of the team's outputs are sent to the Opportunities To Improve Team in Provincial House - either by mail or by E-mail. Here the outputs from all teams are entered into a database from which reports can be produced on specified topics.

The monthly *"Understanding Process Update"* is one of the reports and it is available either in its entirety, or in sections, to all teams as a tool to facilitate improvement. It

DOCUMENT No: 3.13	Organisation	National and Provincial Building Society
	Document	Understanding process (p5)

is able to serve this function as it can readily be seen from the document which issues have been raised against particular teams and topics, and indeed by whom they were raised as well as when.

Much learning can also be gained from seeing the pattern of issues over time - which have risen in size, which have diminished, which have gone away, and which recur on a cyclical basis. This view of the issues database is called the *"Issueometer"* - because it meters or measures issues. Again this is available to teams on request.

The issues database is used to compile the *Top Organisational Issues* which are considered by DMP each month. These are issues which are of particular importances either because of their size, their significance of their longevity. The responses to these issues appear as a DMP output in the Aide Memoire.

Customer Feedback also forms part of our understanding - of where improvement or achievement is occurring. Such feedback is sent to the Opportunities To Improve Team by players engaging with customers where it is entered into the Customer Feedback Database. Reports created from this database are a rich source of potential improvement requirements for teams around the organisation.

OTHER METHODS FOR SHARING UNDERSTANDING

Understanding events and Aide Memoires are not the only methods we use to share understanding. They are supported by a variety of other documents:

Weekly Bulletin
♦ Provides understanding of an operational or procedural nature

Special Bulletin
♦ Shares more detailed understanding of an operational or procedural nature

Focus Magazine
♦ Conveys more informal understanding about our players and teams

Programme Understanding Document
♦ Supplies understanding of our Customer Requirements Programmes

Understanding Documents (e.g. Direction Document, Annual Plan)
♦ Gives more detailed understanding of aspects of our Direction to support the articulation at understanding events, and provides a permanent record for players

Letters from Alastair Lyons
♦ A means of sharing important directional understanding with players when speed is of the essence. A pre-cursor to discussion at understanding events.

DOCUMENT No: 3.13   Document   Understanding process (p6)
Organisation   National and Provincial Building Society

Whilst all of the above should be understandable in their own right, they should all be seen as potential inputs to team events where understanding can be developed further.

DOCUMENT No: 3.13

Organisation National and Provincial
Building Society
Document Understanding process (p7)

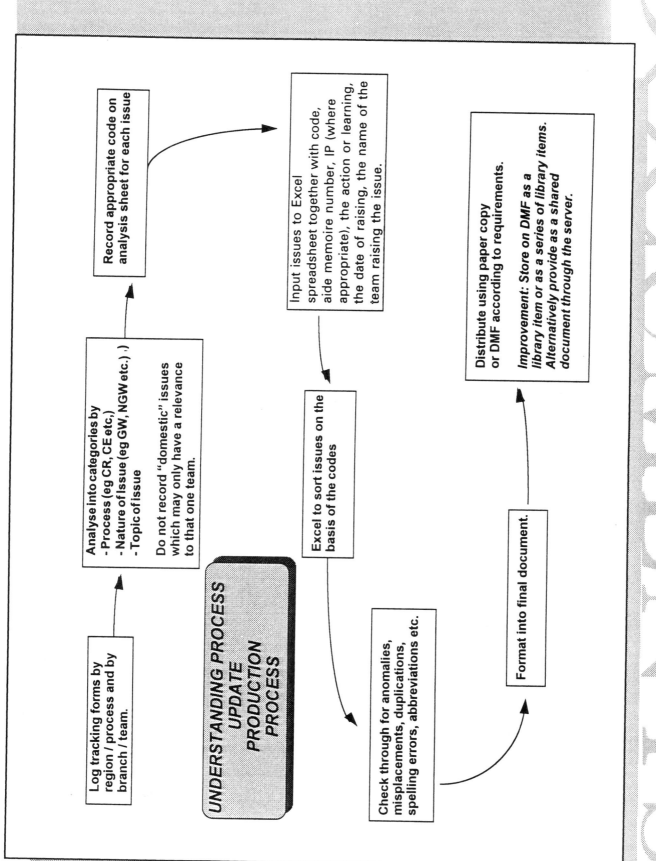

Record appropriate code on analysis sheet for each issue

Input issues to Excel spreadsheet together with code, aide memoire number, IP (where appropriate), the action or learning, the date of raising, the name of the team raising the issue.

Distribute using paper copy or DMF according to requirements.

*Improvement: Store on **DMF** as a library item or as a series of library items. Alternatively provide as a shared document through the server.*

Analyse into categories by
- Process (eg CR, CE etc,)
- Nature of Issue (eg GW, NGW etc.))
- Topic of issue

Do not record "domestic" issues which may only have a relevance to that one team.

Excel to sort issues on the basis of the codes

Log tracking forms by region / process and by branch / team.

*UNDERSTANDING PROCESS
UPDATE
PRODUCTION
PROCESS*

Format into final document.

Check through for anomalies, misplacements, duplications, spelling errors, abbreviations etc.

DOCUMENTS

DOCUMENT No: 3.13

Document   Understanding process (p8)

Organisation   National and Provincial Building Society

ISSUEOMETER - April 1996

Issueometer 23
18/04/96

Key:

< > = Gone well raised by less than 5 teams
* = Gone wells raised by approx 10 teams
** = Gone wells raised by approx 10 - 20 teams
*** = Gone wells raised by approx 20+ teams

< > = Gone well raised by less than 5 teams
= Not gone well, issues and concerns raised by approx 10 teams
= Not gone wells, issues and concerns raised by approx 10 - 20 teams
= Not gone wells, issues and concerns raised by approx 20+ teams

		Mar-96	Feb-96	Jan-96	Dec-95	Nov-95	Oct-95	Sep-95	Aug-95	Jul-95	Jun-95	May-95	Apr-95	Mar-95	Feb-95	Jan-95
RRC	**Planned Pay:**															
	* Well received	*	**													
PAD	**Competency Assessments**															
	# Concerns re Competency Assessments in 1996, no documentation available				#											
	Reward & Processing															
	* Reward in 1996 - contribution better recognised / managed within lifmescales	*														
	# Concern at having to submit reward proposals before Understanding shared by DMP		#													
PAD	**Payroll**															
	# Processing problems with August payroll								#							
PAD	**Recruitment:**															
	#2 No response to adverts and newly recruited players declining employment due to merger speculation.							#								
	#3 Concerns that Reeds are not fully meeting our requirements re temporary players	< >										#				
RRC	**Choices:**															
	# More clarity on Inland Revenue position on Benefit in Kind/Mortgages		< >	< >												
	# Players not being able to choose extra holiday		#													

1   I:\SAPR96.XLS
14:08 22/04/96

4 evaluating effectiveness

In a fast moving business, there is always the temptation to move on to the next priority as soon as the previous one has been actioned. Unless evaluation takes place, it is not possible to assess accurately the contribution that has been made towards achieving business results, to plan the next stage efficiently, or to learn and to improve.

Effective evaluation requires clear, measurable objectives, a robust data gathering process to build a picture of what change has occurred as a result of a set of actions, and the commitment to put learning points into action. Tools such as surveys and focus groups are used both to evaluate effectiveness and to identify future needs. A number of the examples in Chapter Two are therefore also relevant to evaluation.

Objective Evaluation

- Evaluation is vital. Without it, it's impossible to plan for future success. But an Investors in People assessor recently commented that it is the area in which most companies seem to be weak.

- Evaluation is only possible where clear objectives exist. Each communications strategy and plan should specify — in measurable terms — what it aims to achieve.

- Having clear links between business and communication objectives, and ensuring that the communication objectives are measurable, will help to make sure that the value of communication is recognised.

- There are various levels of evaluating the effectiveness of communication:
  - have people received the communication: are the channels effective? how good are managers' communication skills?
  - have people understood it?
  - have they internalised it — in other words, will they act differently as a result?

— is what is being communicated through actions and words consistent?
— what is the quality of two-way communication? are comments and ideas acted on or ignored?

- Make sure you are clear on what each of your communication processes are there to deliver. Are they there to consult? to motivate? to inform? to train? to gather feedback? to negotiate? Are they fulfilling their purpose? Clarity on the aim of each process will mean you can measure whether or not you are achieving success.

- Tools for measuring the effectiveness of communication include the qualitative — focus groups, telephone research, etc. — and quantitative written questionnaires. Surveys are often used both to understand how effective a programme has been, and to identify future needs. See the section in Chapter Two on needs identification tools for more detail.

- Make sure that every communication mechanism includes an integral feedback process to help monitor effectiveness. One company uses regular cross-functional discussion groups to build understanding of core strategies. After each session, group leaders are asked to fill in a feedback form listing unanswered questions, issues, plus any comments on the effectiveness of the communication. They also have the opportunity to attend a leaders' feedback session to give feedback direct — both about the subject, and the effectiveness of the process. This information is analysed by the communication team and amendments made on an ongoing basis.

- Use quantitative tools to measure the number of people who have received the communication. Alternatively, you may be able to build in ongoing monitoring of receipt into the communication process itself. This could be as simple as getting people to complete signing in sheets for major presentations. Electronic news-sheets may have a facility for checking the number of times a story has been accessed.

- Evaluating the extent to which a message has been understood is often easier to do through focus groups. Questions can be used to probe understanding gently through discussing the topic with the group — and to discover how they feel about it. Use of written questionnaires to do the same thing can make the person answering feel as though they are taking an exam!

- Evaluating the extent to which people have internalised the message is easier where there are specific behaviours which the company wants to encourage. Post Office Counters are diversifying the services that they offer their customers. A wide range of products now includes, for example, holiday insurance cover and an exchange service. A campaign was initiated to encourage staff to cross-sell — pro-actively suggesting other services to customers. The communication programme included an explanation of the rationale. Subsequently, regular customer research, carried out by MORI, was used to identify the extent to which such suggestions were being made.

- Measure people's perception of the fit between the messages they hear, and the behaviours and actions they see around them. Where there are discrepancies put them high on the remedial action plan.

- Build in an evaluation stage at the end of every project incorporating a communication element — and make sure it happens! The pace of business life means that it is all too easy for this final stage to get missed or put on ice, so that valuable learning opportunities are missed. Think through how the learning one team has gained can be shared with others.

- If you have a communication steering group, use it as part of the evaluation process. The group can play an important role in assessing feedback and other data and making recommendations for improvement. Members can also gather feedback from colleagues on a formal or informal basis. Take care though that suggested improvements are owned on a broad basis by people who will need to implement them, rather than by a few key individuals.

- Using a range of evaluation tools will ensure the most robust understanding of effectiveness. BT combines an annual quantitative survey with qualitative techniques. The CARE survey covers a broad range of topics with core questions on communication asked on an annual basis to allow tracking. Focus groups, run by managers, are also regularly used. The company also employs an outside agency to carry out omnibus surveys — literally, stopping people on their way out of the building to ask questions about recent communications to test levels of recall and understanding.

- Telephone research can also be used to monitor reaction to a sensitive announcement. A question sheet used in this way by the Inland Revenue is included in the documentation section.

A barometer group can be a good way of informally tracking effectiveness on an ongoing basis. Jane Mullins of Cable and Wireless Business Networks has identified a number of individuals across the business whom she regularly calls to gather reactions to communication. Carefully chosen to reflect a spread of experience and attitudes, they include both people who are champions of change, and others who are resistant to it.

Where communication issues are raised in a particular part of the business, Jane asks a member of the group to probe further so that the root cause can be properly understood and addressed.

- Encourage people in the organisation to evaluate the effectiveness of communication for themselves, as part of the process of establishing ownership for communication where it belongs — with people throughout the business. The National and Provincial Building Society has team appraisals, where team members evaluate the effectiveness of all their processes, including communication.

- Self appraisal — combined with a 360 degree feedback process — can be a powerful mechanism for change. Where managers are asked to assess their own effectiveness at communicating against the effectiveness of others, a common result appears to be that each individual rates their own skills more highly than that of their colleagues! Once managers are made aware of this pattern, the need for change is understood.

- Evaluation needs to be followed by action. Make sure that you have processes in place to implement the learning points you have identified — so that you can create a virtuous circle of continuously improving communications.

Documents in this section

DOCUMENT No: 4.1 Organisation AA	Document Description	Satisfaction Questionnaire Questionnaire distributed to participants at management meetings (p1)

SATISFACTION QUESTIONNAIRE

OPEN MANAGEMENT MEETINGS

We would like to know how useful today's Meeting has been for you. Your views will help us to improve future Meetings. Please take a few minutes to answer the questions below.

1. The purpose of today's Meeting has been to provide an opportunity for you to discuss issues important to the AA, to you and to your team. How well do you think this has been achieved?

    Very well   *Quite well*   *Not very well*   *Not at all well*

2. How useful have you found today's Meeting?

    Very useful   *Useful*   *Not very useful*   *Not at all useful*

3. How satisfied were you with the answers given to questions raised?

    Very satisfied   *Satisfied*   *Not very satisfied*   *Not at all satisfied*

4. Do you think the Meeting focused on the key issues facing the AA?

    Yes   *Partly*   *No*

5. After today's Meeting you are asked to brief your teams (you will receive a summary of the issues discussed today). How useful do you think such a briefing will be for your team?

    Very useful   *Useful*   *Not very useful*   *Not at all useful*

6. Did today's Meeting encourage you to have your say?   *Yes*   *No*

7. Would you like to attend further Meetings like today's?   *Yes*   *No*

8. What were the most valuable aspects of today?

DOCUMENT No: 4.1
Organisation   AA

Document   Satisfaction Questionnaire
(p2)

9. How could the Meeting have been improved?

10. Any other comments?

Thank you for completing this questionnaire. **Please return it before you leave.
Or, send it to**   **Floor 2A, Norfolk House, Basingstoke.**

DOCUMENT No: 4.2	Document	Communications Forum Questionnaire
Organisation Lombard Personal Finance	Description	Questionnaire distributed to participants of Forum meeting between cross-functional staff and managing director (p1)

Communications Forum Questionnaire

31st January 1996

1. Did you willingly put your name forward to attend the forum?

2. Prior to the forum, did you know who John Morgan was?

3. Prior to the forum, did you know anything of Personal Sector outside your own business unit?

4. Did you find the forum useful (on scale of 1–5 — one being absolutely not, five being excellent) for:

    Information about Lombard Group

    Information about Personal Sector

    Information about your own business unit

    Finding out from the other participants what was going on in their part of the business

    Meeting John Morgan

    Having your views heard

5. Can you identify the four business units that make up Personal Sector?

6. Do you think it is important that you know the answer to No 5?

7. Would you recommend attendance at a communication forum to any of your colleagues:

DOCUMENT No: 4.2

Organisation   Lombard Personal Finance

Document   Communications Forum
Questionnaire (p2)

8.   Do you find information about Personal Sector, Lombard Group and our parent
NatWest useful: Please tick most appropriate answer.

Yes, definitely
Sometimes
It confuses me when I should be focused on my business unit
Irrelevant

Any further comment? . . . . . .

DOCUMENT No: 4.3	Document	Telephone Survey Example
Organisation Inland Revenue	Description	Survey form used when contacting random selection of employees to monitor reactions to a sensitive message

Telephone Survey Example

What is your immediate reaction to the article on ----------------------------------?

What are the reactions of your colleagues ?

Does the article answer your initial questions ?

Is there anything you think hasn't been covered ?

How do you feel about the implications for you ?

Do you think the article was honest ?

Do you think there is something you are not being told ?

What about the style of the article ?

a) easy to read
b) bland
c) too long/short
d) too much /too little information
e) well set out

Anything else you would like to add ?

DOCUMENT No: 4.4

Description Audit Form (p1)

Organisation Royal Mail
Document Effective Leadership Feedback

Effective Leadership Feedback

Notes for completing the questionnaire - *Please use black ink*

Whilst completing the questionnaire please keep in mind that all questions and answers to them should relate specifically to the manager being assessed.

Each question is written in such a way that an 'Agree Strongly' marking is always favourable whilst a 'Disagree Strongly' marking indicates a behaviour capable of perceived improvement.

The marking scale is as follows

- 1 = Disagree Strongly
- 2 = Disagree
- 3 = Agree
- 4 = Agree Strongly
- 0 = Not enough evidence to mark

Circle the number that best describes how you feel about each statement.

Only circle '0' if you have NO OPINION or if the statement DOES NOT APPLY TO YOU or if the statement is NOT CLEAR or if YOU DON'T KNOW

Be honest.

 Please complete the questionnaire on your own.

 When you have completed the questionnaire please return it in the addressed envelope provided by the date agreed with your team leader.

 The process is confidential - no one will know individual markings of team members.

 Your team leader believes the responses given by you and your colleagues will help them improve their performance as a leader, with subsequent benefits to you.

 Thank you for your help.

NAME OF LEADER .... **Ref. No** ....

IF YOU ARE THE LEADER PLEASE TICK BOX ☐

Applying the following rating scale, indicate to what extent you agree or disagree with the statements below:

1	2	3	4	0
Disagree Strongly	Disagree	Agree	Agree Strongly	Not enough evidence to mark

I as team leader do OR the leader of my team does:

VISION

The leader of this team does:

1.	provide a clear and exciting vision consistent with the Mission and Values of Royal Mail	1	2	3	4	0
2.	communicate how the vision translates into stretching goals	1	2	3	4	0

COMMITMENT

The leader of this team does:

3.	take on ownership of ideas adopted by the Business whatever the prior debate	1	2	3	4	0
4.	demonstrate commitment by allocating resources and personal time in support of goals	1	2	3	4	0
5.	lead and involve the team in the process of change	1	2	3	4	0

DOCUMENT No: 4.4	Organisation Document	Royal Mail Effective Leadership Feedback (p2)

MANAGEMENT APPROACH - PEOPLE

The leader of this team does:

6.	frequently recognise work well done	1	2	3	4	0
7.	involve the team in the decision making process	1	2	3	4	0
8.	agree clear objectives consistent with the abilities of the team	1	2	3	4	0
9.	take decisions	1	2	3	4	0
10.	encourage a climate of openness and trust	1	2	3	4	0
11.	demonstrate respect for individuals	1	2	3	4	0
12.	support personal development and training	1	2	3	4	0
13.	encourage and value personal feedback	1	2	3	4	0
14.	challenge unacceptable behaviour	1	2	3	4	0
15.	encourage creativity and innovation	1	2	3	4	0

MANAGEMENT APPROACH - BUSINESS PERFORMANCE

The leader of this team does:

16.	place emphasis on providing added value to customers	1	2	3	4	0
17.	set high work standards	1	2	3	4	0
18.	encourage continuous performance improvements	1	2	3	4	0
19.	measure performance and provide useful feedback	1	2	3	4	0
20.	encourage cross-functional working	1	2	3	4	0

MANAGEMENT APPROACH - PERSONAL CONTRIBUTION

The leader of this team does:

21.	have personal contact with external customers	1	2	3	4	0
22.	display competence and sound judgement	1	2	3	4	0
23.	display integrity and a caring attitude	1	2	3	4	0
24.	ensure a high level of visibility and accessibility	1	2	3	4	0
25.	accept personal accountability	1	2	3	4	0

COMMUNICATION

The leader of this team does:

26.	seize opportunities to communicate business policies effectively	1	2	3	4	0
27.	frequently use face-to-face communication	1	2	3	4	0
28.	seek input and listen	1	2	3	4	0
29.	provide information on the unit's performance on a regular basis	1	2	3	4	0
30.	practise open, honest and positive communication	1	2	3	4	0

I report directly to the person in question (please tick only one box)   Yes ☐   No ☐

How long have you been working together as a team with this leader? (please tick only one box)   Less than 6 months ☐   More than 6 months ☐

Now, please choose from the questions the most important to you and note the numbers in the boxes below.

By "most important to you" we are asking you to indicate those behaviours which YOU consider to be the most important in an effective leader.

☐   ☐   ☐   ☐   ☐   ☐

THANK YOU FOR COMPLETING THIS QUESTIONNAIRE

DOCUMENTS

DOCUMENT No: 4.4

Document   Effective Leadership Feedback (p3)

Organisation   Royal Mail

SUMMARY OF BAROMETER GROUP FEEDBACK

PCP:

GROUP LEADER

AREA: CONTENT   SCORE FOR CONTENT (1–5) _____

How much information did the face-to-face briefing provide me with that allowed me to understand what the Employee Agenda is about?

Key points raised:

What reason in the face-to-face briefing helped me understand why the Employee Agenda is essential for the future of Royal Mail?

Key points raised:

What in the face-to-face briefing convinced me that the Employee agenda is fair for employees? If it didn't, why not?

Key points raised:

What can I now talk confidently and positively about the Employee Agenda with my team and local reps? What else do I need?

Key points raised:

DOCUMENT No: 4.5

Organisation Royal Mail Anglia
Document Summary of Barometer Group Feedback (p1)

SUMMARY OF BAROMETER GROUP FEEDBACK

PCP:

GROUP LEADER: _____

AREA: COMPREHENSIVENESS   SCORE FOR COMPREHENSIVENESS (1–5) _____

What gaps/questions has the information I have received so far left me with? List the incidences

Key points raised:

AREA: TIMELINESS   SCORE FOR TIMELINESS (1–5) _____

Had you already received the information contained in the briefings from other sources? If so what were they?

Key points raised\;

DOCUMENT No: 4.5

Organisation Royal Mail Anglia

Document   Summary of Barometer Group
Feedback (p2)

SUMMARY OF BAROMETER GROUP FEEDBACK

PCP:

GROUP LEADER:

AREA: OVERALL SATISFACTION   SCORE FOR OVERALL SATISFACTION (1–5) _____

Do you as managers feel sufficiently involved in the Employee Agenda communication?

Key points raised:

Are you able to talk with confidence about it to your team?

Key points raised:

OTHER AREAS FOR DISCUSSION

What improvements would you like in future communications?

What else are you getting information from on the
Employee Agenda? what is it saying? Which do you listen to most and why?

Are there any issues relating to the Employee Agenda you would like addressing?

DOCUMENT No: 4.5 Organisation Royal Mail Anglia
Document   Guidelines for Feedback (p1)

EMPLOYEE *agenda*
GUIDELINES FOR FEEDBACK
(MANAGERS - No. 8: week commencing 11/12/95)

Employee Agenda Update (dated 1 December 1995)

~ How useful did you find the Employee Agenda Update which you received last
week?

~ How far did the Update provide you with the information you need to speak
confidently about Employee Agenda with your employees?

~ Are your employees aware that Employee Agenda and pay negotiations are distinct,
and that the Employee Agenda negotiations *will* continue?

~ How useful were the explanations in the Update of why the whole Employee
Agenda, and pay restructuring in particular, are so important?

Overall satisfaction with the Update: *(please circle one)*

1	2	3	4	5
poor		acceptable		excellent

DOCUMENT No: 4.5
Organisation   Royal Mail Anglia

Document   Guidelines for Feedback (p2)

General Satisfaction

- Are your Employee Agenda queries being answered satisfactorily between briefings?

- Are there any major or obvious misconceptions about Employee Agenda among employees which you think need to be addressed?

- What improvements could be made to improve future communication between briefings?

Overall satisfaction with communications so far:

1	2	3	4	5
not at all		fairly		completely

OTHER COMMENTS

Please include any other comments you wish to make on the communications to date: including problems with particular subject areas; in particular offices/functions; or any suggestions or approval for divisional communications or best practice.

DOCUMENT No: 4.5
Organisation   Royal Mail Anglia

Document   Current methods of Communication
              within unit
Description   Checklist used with line managers
              to evaluate effectiveness of local
              communications (p1)

CURRENT METHODS OF COMMUNICATION WITHIN UNIT.

	✓	Comments.
Team Briefings.		
Notice Boards.		
Electronic Displays.		
Letters to Employees.		
Office Newsletter.		
Manager Meetings. *		
Focus Groups. *		
Quality Guidance Group. *		
Employee * Satisfaction Group.		
Bright Ideas. *		
Understanding the Business.		

*Are the outputs communicated ? If so how ?

DOCUMENT No: 4.5
Organisation   Royal Mail Anglia

Document   Current methods of Communication
within unit (p2)

TEAM BRIEFING

MANAGER QUESTIONNAIRE

How often do you conduct a Team Briefing ?	
When was the last one held ?	
How much notice are you given by your Manager of when a Briefing will take place ?	
Where are they held ?	
What items are discussed ?	
How long do the sessions last ?	
Do you provide an opportunity for questions ?	
How do you give feedback ?	
Any other comments ?	

DOCUMENTS

DOCUMENT No: 4.5

Organisation Royal Mail Anglia
Document   Current methods of Communication
within unit (p3)

TEAM BRIEFING

EMPLOYEE QUESTIONNAIRE

How often do you attend a Team Briefing ?	
When was the last one held ?	
How much notice are you given of when a briefing will take place ?	
Where are they held ?	
What items are discussed ?	
How long do the sessions last ?	
Is there an opportunity for you to ask questions ?	
How is feedback given ?	
Any other comments ?	

DOCUMENTS

NOTICE BOARD GUIDELINES

	✓	Comments.
Has the Notice Board "Ownership" ?		
Has the Notice Board a "Header" ?		
Is the Notice Board up-to-date ?		
Is the Notice Board "User Friendly" ?		
Any other comments ?		

DOCUMENT No: 4.5

Organisation   Royal Mail Anglia
Document   Current methods of
                Communication within unit (p5)

INFORMATION DISPLAYS

TITLE OF DISPLAY	✓ or ✗	OBSERVATIONS
Business Mission & Values.		
Health & Safety at Work Act.		
Safe Systems of Work.		
Alert States.		
Evacuation Procedures.		
Fire Action & Assembly Points.		
COSHH Regulations.		
How to Deal with Suspect Packages.		
Hypodermic Needles Found Loose.		
First Aider(s) on Duty.		
Occupational Health Service Contact.		
Welfare Officer.		
Harassment Policy Statement.		
Quality of Service Results.		
Employee Opinion Survey Results.		
Environment Policy Statement.		
Leadership Charter.		

Note: Is the Information up-to-date and user friendly ?

DOCUMENTS

DOCUMENT No: 4.5

Organisation   Royal Mail Anglia

Document   Current methods of Communication within unit (p6)

RECOMMENDATIONS

PROCESSES	PEOPLE
(Team Briefing structure, Newsletter, Notice Board layout, Written Communication, Meetings.)	(Writing Effectively, Presentation Skills, Listening Skills, Benchmarking, Managing Meetings)

DOCUMENT No: 4.5

Organisation
Document

Royal Mail Anglia
Current methods of
Communication within unit (p7)

COMMUNICATIONS IMPROVEMENT PLAN

OBJECTIVE	ACTIVITIES	LEAD ROLE	SUPPORT	MEASUREMENT	TARGET DATE FOR COMPLETION

DOCUMENTS

5 getting the most from external consultants

The last few years have seen a great expansion in the number of consultancies offering their services within the internal communication and broader HR field. Used effectively, consultants can be an invaluable aid for the internal communicator yet used carelessly they can be a time consuming and costly mistake. To ensure that you are getting the most from consultants you use, consider the following key areas:

— what can they add?

— how can you work with them to get the best results?

What can they add?

- Consultants can offer:
  - knowledge and expertise: a thorough understanding of internal communication, current ideas and practice
  - experience as to what is being done in other sectors, markets and organisations
  - practical experience in developing processes and implementing their components

- consultants can provide an independent view point, offering a fresh eye on an issue with no organisational baggage. Using their experience, consultants are able to guide and help your thinking. Often their experience and understanding of other organisations and practices help consultants analyse your specific issues, circumstances, problems and requirements with greater objectivity. They can often predict the potential pitfalls of certain courses of action.

- consultants are able to bring new skills and complement those existing internally. These skills can be employed only as required, obviating the need to employ extra staff to conduct a particular project. They can be replaced relatively easily to ensure freshness of approach, or if their skills no longer reflect the needs of the job in hand.

- In some circumstances consultants are useful in researching sensitive issues and presenting data in a less threatening way than if coming from internal sources. Consultants are often better placed than internal staff to challenge existing practices, beliefs or approaches and elicit a more constructive response.

Working with consultants

- Once you have decided that consultants do have a role to play in your particular initiative, it is important to select them well and decide the terms upon which you will do business with them. Some tips here are:
  - select an appropriate consultancy. In some cases a smaller local outfit may be more appropriate than a larger (and more expensive!) concern
  - ask for references from others for whom the consultants have worked. Ideally, chat with a few of the referees over the phone
  - where possible, build the consultants into a combined internal/external project team. This may well be more cost effective and will help ensure a bespoke approach. It could also prevent others in your organisation from thinking that a body of expensive consultants are waltzing in, forcefitting one of their processes, and then waltzing out again, as some may be tempted to believe
  - always make sure that consultants have a clear point of contact capable of making decisions
  - do not be afraid to buy the occasional day's thinking from a consultant. They do not always have to work on long projects with you
  - where possible, work with consultants to transfer their skills to sustain a project in-house. This can save money and reinforce the feeling of ownership.

- As the project takes shape you can ensure that your relationship with a consultant is most productive if you:
  - outline constraints and all relevant information straightaway, or as soon as they emerge
  - give clear direction and welcome constructive feedback from the consultant as to its quality
  - regularly monitor progress and expect updates, though try not to hector
  - at the outset, agree upon the time required for a project and its costs as well as how either of these should be reviewed, if necessary.

bibliography

Communication skills: a practical handbook
Industrial Society, London, 1993

The effective communicator   John Adair
Industrial Society, London

Influencing Communication   Liz Cochrane
A practitioner's guide to internal communication consultancy
The Industrial Society, 1997

Communications for managers: a practical handbook
Industrial Society, London, 1993

Team briefing   Phil McGeough
Industrial Society, London, 1995

Joint consultation   Roger Moores
Industrial Society, London, 1995

Managing transitions   William Bridges
Nicholas Brealey, London, 1995

Gower handbook of internal communication
Editor: Eileen Scholes
Gower, Aldershot, 1997

Communication: why managers must do more
Researched by Dr Jon White; written and published by Hedron Consulting Ltd,
London

Communication futures: technology
Smythe Dorward Lambert, London 1994

The rise to power of the corporate communicator
Smythe Dorward Lambert, London, 1991

The power of the open company
Smythe Dorward Lambert, London, 1991

Corporate reputation: managing the new strategic asset
Smythe Dorward Lambert, London, 1993

Communication futures: empowerment – any life left?
Smythe Dorward Lambert, London, 1996

The communicating organisation
Michael Blakstad and Dr Aldwyn Cooper
IPD, London, 1995

Consultancy: understanding the dynamics
South Bank University International Consulting Conference, London, 1994

Process consultation Volumes 1 and 2
Ed Schein
Addison Wesley Publishing Company, Harlow, 1987

Articulate executive: orchestrating effective communication
Harvard Business School Press, Harvard USA, 1994

Communicating change
T.J. Larkin and Sandar Larkin
McGraw-Hill Inc, New York USA, 1994

Are managers getting the message?
Institute of Management, Corby, 1993

How to be a great communicator: the complete guide to mastering internal
communication   David M. Martin
Institute of Management/Pitman, London, 1995

Communicating corporate change: practical guide to communication and
corporate strategy   B. Quirke
McGraw-Hill, Maidenhead, 1996

Strategic organisational communication   C. Conrad
Holt Rinehart and Wilson, USA, 1990

Organisational communication for survival
V.P. Richmond and J.C. McCroskey
Prentice Hall, Hemel Hempstead, 1991

Fundamentals of organisational communication
P. Shockley-Zalabak
Longman, Harlow, 1995